Saving Lives

Saving Lives

POEMS

Albert Goldbarth

Ohio State University Press   Columbus

Library of Congress Cataloging-in-Publication Data
Goldbarth, Albert.
Saving lives : poems / Albert Goldbarth.
p.   cm.
ISBN 0-8142-0871-1 (alk. paper) —
ISBN 0-8142-5073-4 (pbk. : alk. paper)
I. Title.
PS3557.O354 S28   2001
811'.54—dc21   00-047867

Text and jacket design by Paula Newcomb.
Type set in Electra by Tseng Information Systems, Inc.
Printed by Thomson-Shore, Inc.

The paper used in this publication meets the minimum requirements
of the American National Standard for Information Sciences—
Permanence of Paper for Printed Library Materials.
ANSI Z39.48-1992.

9 8 7 6 5 4 3 2 1

ACKNOWLEDGMENTS

The author is grateful to the editors of the following journals, where the poems of this collection first appeared:

Library: *The Iowa Review*
Into the Lives of Other People: *The Gettysburg Review*
Power of Weirdness: *The Ontario Review*
1880: *The Ohio Review*
Second Thoughts: *Boulevard*
Poem Spoken by a Plaque at Scenic View: *Western Humanities Review*
Sestina: As There Are Support Groups . . . : *The Paris Review*
A Conjugal Beauty: *The Bellingham Review*
Canceling Out: *Boulevard*
Astronomy: *The Iowa Review*
. . . one of whom had apparently died in childbirth: *Poetry*
The Hardy Boys' Detective Handbook (1959): *The Gettysburg Review*
Glass: *Quarterly West*
The Geese: *Poetry*
Transplanting: *The Ontario Review*
A Continuum: *The Beloit Poetry Journal*
Won't Let Go: *The Georgia Review*
Sung Grievously: *Western Humanities Review*
Reentry: *The Southwest Review*
Rembrandt / Panties: *Boulevard*
A Photo of a Lover from My Junior Year in College: *Boulevard*
Goliath and the Barbarians: The Georgia Review
Invisible: *Quarterly West*
Canyon, Gorge, Arroyo: *Poetry*
A Cup: *The Georgia Review*
Suitcase Song: *Poetry*
Rarefied: *Poetry*
Zenith: *The Ohio Review*
The Great Ones: *The Iowa Review*
Ecstasy,: *The Ohio Review*

Her Literal One: *The Georgia Review* (and reprinted in *The Pushcart Prize XXV*)
January 31, 1998: *The Kenyon Review*

―――――――

Thanks to Nathan, for the snapping eye; and Skyler, for the helping hand.

CONTENTS

Library

Library

This book saved my life.

This book takes place on one of the two small tagalong moons of Mars.

This book requests its author's absolution, centuries after his death.

This book required two of the sultan's largest royal elephants to bear it; this other book fit in a gourd.

This book reveals The Secret Name of God, and so its author is on a death list.

This is the book I lifted high over my head, intending to smash a roach in my girlfriend's bedroom; instead, my back unsprung, and I toppled painfully into her bed, where I stayed motionless for eight days.

This is a "book." That is, an audiocassette. This other "book" is a screen and a microchip. This other "book," the sky.

In chapter 3 of this book, a woman tries explaining her husband's tragically humiliating death to their daughter: reading it is like walking through a wall of setting cement.

This book taught me everything about sex.

This book is plagiarized.

This book is transparent; this book is a codex in Aztec; this book, written by a prisoner, in dung; the wind is turning the leaves of this book: a hill-top olive as thick as a Russian novel.

This book is a vivisected frog, and ova its text.

This book was dictated by Al-Méllikah, the Planetary Spirit of the Seventh Realm, to his intermediary on Earth (the Nineteenth Realm), who published it, first in mimeograph, and many editions later in gold-stamped leather.

This book taught me everything wrong about sex.

This book poured its colors into my childhood so strongly they remain a dye in my imagination today.

This book is by a poet who makes me sick.

This is the first book in the world.

This is a photograph from Vietnam, titled "Buddhist nuns copying scholarly Buddhist texts in the pagoda."

This book smells like salami.

This book is continued in volume 2.

He was driving—evidently by some elusive, interior radar, since he was busy reading a book propped on the steering wheel.

This book picks on men.

This is the split Red Sea: two *heavy* pages.

In this book I underlined *deimos, cabochon, pelagic, hegira*. I wanted to use them.

This book poured its bile into my childhood.

This book defames women.

This book was smuggled into the country one page at a time, in tiny pill containers, in hatbands, in the cracks of asses; sixty people risked their lives repeatedly over this one book.

This book is nuts!!!

This book cost more than a seven-story chalet in the Tall Oaks subdivision.

This book—I don't remember.

This book is a hoax, and a damnable lie.

This chapbook was set in type and printed by hand, by Larry Levis's then-wife, the poet Marcia Southwick, in 1975. It's 1997 now and Larry's dead—too early, way too early—and this elliptical, heartbreaking poem (which is, in part, exactly *about* too early death) keeps speaking to me from its teal-green cover: the way they say the nails and the hair continue to grow in the grave.

This book is two wings and a thorax the size of a sunflower seed.

This book gave me a hard-on.

This book is somewhere under those other books way over there.

This book deflected a bullet.

This book provided a vow I took.

If they knew you owned this book, they'd come and get you; it wouldn't be pretty.

This book is a mask: its author isn't anything like it.

This book is by William Matthews, a *wonderful* poet, who died today, age fifty-five. Now Larry Levis has someone he can talk to.

This book is an "airplane book" (but not *about* airplanes; meant *to be read on* an airplane; also, available every three steps in the airport). What does it mean, to "bust" a "block"?

This is the book I pretended to read one day in the Perry-Castañeda Library browsing room, but really I was rapt in covert appreciation of someone in a slinky skirt that clung like kitchen plasticwrap. She squiggled near and pointed to the book. "It's upside-down," she said.

For the rest of the afternoon I was so flustered that when I finally left the library . . . this is the book, with its strip of magnetic-code tape, that I absentmindedly walked with through the security arch on the first day of its installation, becoming the first (though unintentional) light-fingered lifter of books to trigger the Perry-Castañeda alarm, which hadn't been fine-tuned as yet, and sounded even louder than the sirens I remember from grade school air-raid drills, when the principal had us duck beneath our desks and cover our heads—as if gabled —with a book.

The chemical formulae for photosynthesis: this book taught me that.

And this book taught me what a "merkin" is.

The cover of this book is fashioned from the tanned skin of a favorite slave.

This book is inside a computer now.

This "book" is made of knotted string; and this, of stone; and this, the gut of a sheep.

This book existed in a dream of mine, and only there.

This book is a talk-show paperback with shiny gold raised lettering on the cover. (Needless to say, not one by me.)

This is a book of prohibitions; this other, a book of rowdy license. They serve equally to focus the prevalent chaos of our lives.

This book is guarded around the clock by men in navy serge and golden braiding, carrying *very* capable guns.

This is the book that destroyed a marriage. Take it, burn it, before it costs us more.

This book is an intercom for God.

This book I slammed against a wall.

My niece wrote this book in crayon and glitter.

This is the book (in a later paperback version) by which they recognized the sea-bleached, battered, and otherwise-unidentifiable body of Shelley.

Shit: I forgot to send in the card, and now the Book Club has billed me *twice* for *Synopses of 400 Little-Known Operas.*

This book is filled with sheep and rabbits, calmly promenading in their tartan vests and bow ties, with their clay pipes, in their Easter Sunday salad-like hats. The hills are gently rounded. The sun is a clear, firm yolk. The world will never be this sweetly welcoming again.

This book is studded with gems that have the liquid depth of aperitifs.

This book, *1,000 Wild Nights,* is actually wired to give an electr/ YOWCH!

This book I stole from Cornell University's Olin Library in the spring of 1976. Presumably, its meter's still running. Presumably, it still longs for its Dewey'd place in the dim-lit stacks.

This book has a bookplate reminding me, in Latin, to use my scant time well.

It's the last day of the semester. My students are waiting to sell their textbooks back to the campus store, like crazed racehorses barely restrained at the starting gate.

This book caused a howl / a stir / a ruckus / an uproar.

This book became a movie; they quickly raised the cover price.

This book is the Key to the Mysteries.

This book has a bookplate: a man and a woman have pretzeled themselves into one lubricious shape.

This book came apart in my hands.

This book is austere; it's like holding a block of dry ice.

This Bible is in Swahili.

This book contains seemingly endless pages of calculus—it may as well be in Swahili.

This is the book I pretended to read while Ellen's lushly naked body darkened into sleep beside me. And *this* is the book I pretended to read in a waiting room once, as a cardiac specialist razored into my father's chest. And THIS book I pretended having read once, when I interviewed for a teaching position: "Oh yes," I said, "of course," and spewed a stream of my justly famous golden bullshit into the conference room.

This book was signed by the author fifteen minutes before she died.

This is Erhard Ratdolf's edition of Johann Regiomontanus's astronomical and astrological calendar (1476)—it contains "the first true title-page."

She snatched this book from a garbage can, just as Time was about to swallow it out of the visible world irrevocably. To this day, her grandchildren read it.

This book: braille. This one: handmade paper, with threads of the poet's own bathrobe as part of the book's rag content. This one: the cover is hollowed glass, with a goldfish swimming around the title.

This is my MFA thesis. Its title is *Goldbarth's MFA Thesis.*

This is the cookbook used by Madame Curie. It still faintly glows, seven decades later.

This book is the shame of an entire nation.

This book is one of fourteen matching volumes, like a dress parade.

This is the book I'm writing now. It's my best! (But where should I send it?)

This book doesn't do anyth/ oh wow, check THIS out!

This is the book I bought for my nephew, *101 Small Physics Experiments.* Later he exchanged it for *The Book of Twerps and Other Pukey Things,* and who could blame him?

This book is completely marred by the handiwork of the *Druckfehlerteufel*—"the imp who supplies the misprints."

This book has a kind of aurora-like glory radiating from it. There should be versions of uranium detectors that register glory-units from books.

We argued over this book in the days of the divorce. I kept it, she kept the stained-glass window from Mike and Mimi.

Yes, he was supposed to be on the 7:05 to Amsterdam. But he stayed at home, to finish this whodunit. And so he didn't crash.

This book has a browned corsage pressed in it. I picked up both for a dime at the Goodwill.

"A diet of berries, vinegar, and goat's milk" will eventually not only cure your cancer, but will allow a man to become impregnated (diagrams explain this)— also, there's serious philosophy about Jews who control "the World Order" in this book.

This book reads from right to left. This book comes with a small wooden top attached by a saffron ribbon. This book makes the sound of a lion, a train, or a cuckoo clock, depending on where you press its cover.

I've always admired this title from 1481: *The Myrrour of the Worlde*.

This book is from the 1950s; the jacket says it's "a doozie."

This book is by me. I found it squealing piteously, poor piglet, in the back of a remainders bin. I took it home and nursed it.

This book let me adventure with the Interplanetary Police.

I threw myself, an aspirant, against the difficult theories this book propounded, until my spirit was bruised. I wasn't any smarter—just bruised.

This book is magic. There's more *inside* it than outside.

This is the copy of the *Iliad* that Alexander the Great took with him, always, on his expeditions—"in," Thoreau says, "a precious casket."

Help! *(thump)* I've been stuck in this book all week and I don't know how to get out! *(thump)*

This is the book of poetry I read from at my wedding to Morgan. We were divorced. The book (Fred Chappell's *River*) is still on my shelf, like an admonishment.

This book is stapled (they're rusted by now); this book, bound in buttery leather; this book's pages are chemically treated leaves; this book, the size of a peanut, is still complete with indicia and an illustrated colophon page.

So tell me: out of what grim institution for the taste-deprived and the sensibility-challenged do they find the cover artists for these books?

This book I tried to carry balanced on my head with seven others.

This book I actually licked.

This book—remember? I carved a large hole in its pages, a "how-to magazine for boys" said this would be a foolproof place to hide my secret treasures. Then I remembered I *didn't have* any secret treasures worth hiding. Plus, I was down one book.

This book is nothing but jackal crap; unfortunately, its royalties have paid for two Rolls-Royces and a mansion in the south of France.

This book is said to have floated off the altar of the church, across the village square, and into the hut of a peasant woman in painful labor.

This is what he was reading when he died. The jacket copy says it's "a real page-turner—you can't put it down!" I'm going to assume he's in another world now, completing the story.

This book hangs by a string in an outhouse, and every day it gets thinner.

This book teaches you how to knit a carrying case for your rosary; this one, how to build a small but lethal incendiary device.

This book has pop-up pages with moveable parts, intended to look like the factory room where pop-up books with moveable parts are made.

If you don't return that book I loaned you, I'm going to smash your face.

This book says the famously saintly woman was really a ring-tailed trash-mouth dirty-down bitch queen. *Everyone's* reading it!

There are stains in this book that carry a narrative greater than its text.

The Case of _____. *How to* _____. Books books books.

I know great petulant stormy swatches and peaceful lulls of this book by heart.

I was so excited, so jazzed up!—but shortly thereafter they found me asleep, over pages 6 and 7 of this soporific book. (I won't say by who.)

And on her way back to her seat, she fell (the multiple sclerosis) and refused all offered assistance. Instead, she used her book she'd been reading from, as a prop, and worked herself pridefully back up to a standing position.

They gave me this book for free at the airport. Its cover features an Indian god with the massive head of an elephant, as brightly blue as a druid, flinging flowers into the air and looking unsurpassably wise.

My parents found this book in my bottom drawer, and spanked the living hell into my butt.

This book of yours, you tell me, was optioned by Hollywood for eighty-five impossibajillion dollars? Oh. Congratulations.

They lowered the esteemed and highly published professor into his grave. A lot of silent weeping. A lot of elegiac rhetoric. And one man shaking his head in the chill December wind dumbfoundedly, who said, "And he perished anyway."

Although my eighth-grade English teacher, Mrs. Hurd, always said, "Whenever you open a book, remember: that author lives again."

After this book, there was no turning back.

Around 1000 A.D., when the Magyars were being converted over to Christianity, Magyar children were forced to attend school for the first time in their cultural history: "therefore the Magyar word *konyv* means tears as well as book."

This book, from when I was five, its fuzzy ducklings, and my mother's voice in the living room of the second-story apartment over the butcher shop on Division Street. . . . I'm fifty now. I've sought out, and I own now, one near-mint and two loose, yellowing copies that mean to me as much as the decorated gold masks and the torsos of marble meant to the excavators of Troy.

This book is done.

This book gave me a paper cut.

This book set its mouth on my heart, and sucked a mottled tangle of blood to the surface.

I open this book and smoke pours out, I open this book and a bad sleet slices my face, I open this book: brass knuckles, I open this book: the spiky scent of curry, I open this book and hands grab forcefully onto my hair as if in violent sex, I open this book: the wingbeat of a seraph, I open this book: the edgy cat-pain wailing of the damned thrusts up in a column as sturdy around as a giant redwood, I open this book: the travel of light, I open this book and it's as damp as a wound, I open this book and I fall inside it farther than any physics, stickier than the jelly we scrape from cracked bones, cleaner than what we tell our children in the dark when they're afraid to close their eyes at night.

And this book can't be written yet: its author isn't born yet.

This book is going to save the world.

Other Lives

Into the Lives of Other People

Half waif, half woman, at fourteen Norma
could target her panhandle pitch *exactly*
(matron, wussy preppie, leering creep)
and live a streethead's version of viable splendor.
"Sunboy taught me meditation that was yoga
laced with acid—he could even shit, or fuck me, in a trance
he called God City—and everything seemed so holy then
in its grubby way, I'd spend a whole day lifting purses
in the Quarter or hustling dollar tricks in portapotties in back
of the go-go bars, and feel saintly. Would you ever—" then
she waves a hand at her good, good life and its very civil
accessories: lovely child, proper mortgage, seemly lawn gazebo

"—guess it?" So it turns out that her feral savvy
was excellent training for managing an advertising agency
(that handles Save Our Kids as a gratis account).
It turns out Chad, the Little-League-coach/lawyer/daddy
in this picture, used to shoot pool over at tumbletown
and gigolo condo widows for a living—"not that this
became the first line of my résumé, you understand."
It turns out, yes, I understand. We
all were at least a dozen successive in utero selves.
It doesn't end: the Me Convention, always
overbooked. (HELLO, My Name Is *Me*. / HELLO,
MY Name Is *Me*. / HELLO, *!MY!* Name. . . .) One night

I said the kinds of things that score the bedroom air with something
unerasable, and a marriage is never the same again . . . is *this*
the man who said those things, the one in the mirror,
here, the one with the pen? . . . In the film *The Elephant Man*,
the kindly doctor looks up from his self-absorptive reverie
—he's swozzled with a little wine—and asks his wife
sincerely, "Am I a good man?—or a bad man?" and
the elemental wrestle of light and shadow over his face
invests his otherwise simple question with a fearful,
and recognizable, profundity. The answer is: we're smugglers,
every one of us, so long as the brain is a living thing, we're smugglers
of uncountable alternate *us*, across the border

and into the lives of other people. I was reading about more
literal contraband (illegal copies of Joyce's *Ulysses*,
and of *Lady Chatterley's Lover*, in a dowager's voluminous skirts;
cocaine as an urn of the dearly departed's ashes;
1996, in Stockholm, a woman was arrested
by customs officers for attempting to smuggle
seventy-five live snakes in her bra: "they had seen her scratching
suspiciously" . . .)—then the phone rang: Chad, to tell us
his case of the week. The man *wasn't* single; the woman
wasn't AIDS-free; the ultra-courteous bellboy was a private eye
and the planter of Wandering Jew was a Japanese microphone.

Power of Weirdness

It was clear that night in 1887, in the barn,
and so when Mrs. Almira Masterson found
this giant yellow dog in the corner
devouring a calf, she dissuaded it
mightily with her broom, and shooed it
into the crisp November darkness, certain of exactly
what she did, and what she did it to—and therefore
swooned the morning after when apprised of her courageous assault
upon Nimrod the lion, escaped from Barnum & Bailey's
winter Bridgeport quarters during the vast,
disastrous conflagration there. It turns out that
no matter how extreme we find a circumstance (and
surely Barnum himself is a sterling example
of *willed* bizarritude: the jerkied "feejee mermaid,"
and the whitewash-rendered "sacred albino pachyderm,"
and his dozens of other zestily-done humbuggeries), we also find
that Life will later ripple it, fillip it, curlicue its dingus
in ways our own belabored piffles of imagination
never could; for instance, when the hoodlum-cronied
(and -monied) City Inspector of Sewers is on his way home
from one more bribe, and out of the lucid blue a block
of frozen pee from flight 1113 fatally smites his pate
—a power of logical weirdness so, *so*
macroscopic we can't see it, like heaven or gravity
or a wisp of the visible universe
suddenly lumping into a nodule or willowing into a sinuosity
in such a way as to knock some cherished
cosmologic gospel on its *tuchus*—Barnum would have understood.
His huge American Museum, five imposing floors on prime-location
Broadway—with its Burmese bull; and Mrs. Nellis,
the "Armless Wonder"; and Chang and Eng, the famous
eponymous Siamese twins; and America's first hippopotamus;
also "not one but two whales"; and, as he put it, "educated dogs,
industrious fleas, automatons, jugglers, living statuary, and soforth"—

was a zoological, *odditological* lily
of a lecture-hall-cum-raree-show you'd think
no man or chance could ever noticeably gild; yet
when *it* burned, July 13 of 1865 (for Barnum was tested
repeatedly by fires), it provided unexpected marvelosity beyond anything
even Barnum's genius snake-oil brain might fancy.
Thousands gathered to gasp. The "Giant Lady" Anna Swan
(at seven feet, eleven inches) needed to be jostled through a smashed-in pane
by derrick. Firemen opened the cages of tropical birds:
"Well kiss me arse" one rookie kept chanting in awe,
a sort of rough-hewn prayer, as cockatoos
and mimicky parrots and macaws and toucans spiraled
through the smoke like a confetti fall in reverse.
A Royal Bengal tiger leaped from the second story, and was axed
to death. A living scribble of snakes
inscribed its uncontested way up Broadway. One ape sauntered
jauntily into the newsroom of the *New York Herald.*
. . . I've thought of this at moments of such smallness
and such quiet that they seem to come from other solar systems
than the one where Barnum ballyhooed his spectacle. But
that's the point, of course: our lives are always maps unfolding
into terra incognita, and a man can watch a woman
curled in after-carnal stillness in their bed, can sense
the easy waves of trust and of satiety she radiates
until the room is comfortably filled with these,
and then she sleeps, and then he curls up next to her, and sleeps . . .
and still it's lions and fires they'll open into, one day,
unexplainably. Say it's six months later,
somewhere along the Madagascar shore
where jungle brambles itself to the very lip of the ocean.
Here, a Madagascar native, on a "spirit wander,"
halts to rest—for four days he's been walking,
with his staff and knife and totems-bag. He knows
a lot—where water can be found beneath plant *this* or *that,*
how far a game cat's cry is, what a god says
in the form of a bird. And so he's very happy
when this vivid green-and-lemon fellow settles in a bough,
announcing "kiss me arse" in a voice that surely
means it's from another world.

1880

These women are alone—the one
whose stare is wide and level,
and the other one, who lids her look
and seems to see a separate world—in Renoir's
At the Concert. They could be named Pro-
and Anti-, they're so different,
although so tied to the rules of the same ocher palette.

    /O/

They're alone, in their elegant theater box, and lost
in the music, whatever the music is
that night, and lost inside whatever other place
the music takes them. But we also know

    /h, I dare say! Excuse me ple/

a century later, the hint of a man
in evening dress has broken through
Renoir's attempt to deeply purplish-umber him
out of existence. Infrared
confirms this, striking through the surface
like a paparazzo seizing on a hidden truth
and lighting it for all time: there's a man,

    /dn't mean to interru/
    /nchanting, my dears. I am suddenl/

or *was* a man, or the faint ghost
or the memory or the prophecy, but
in any case the *presence*, of a man
beneath the artist's failed layers of negation. Or

/istake? No. I refuse to believe
that Chance alone, as opposed
to a Knowing Destiny, has led me here toni/

it might be *they're* the ghostly ones,
to *him*—that they fade out and in like a radio song
in search of its clear point along the megahertz.

/misty to my eyes, don't
leave! Wait! I have much indeed
to tell you, only stay and listen to/

It could be so simple as this: the one who lids her gaze
is dreaming of a lover. Or it could be so amazing
as a spirit from the quantum (and therefore invisible) universe
sundering whatever extradimensional cambium layer keeps
his realm from our familiar, tactile spatiotemporal plane
. . . is it possible

/launched myself in search of, frankly
(my yearnworthy beauties, oh lovely jump-start cables
of my lonely heart) I was, I say, in search
of a different painting to enter altogether, and not,
if you'll forgive such indiscretion, this
complacency of Bach and rosy portraiture.
Listen to me, it's 1880! The telephone is invented!
By four years! Not radio yet, but—wait.
Not laser scanning yet, but—patience. Last year
Albert Einstein was born, and even as I stand here
in your lavish fleshtone ambience (my twin flames
for the moth of my longing), Sigmund Freud
is a lowly and struggling neurologist busy
dissecting crayfish exactly the color of living brick
that the painter has given the walls here
and the plush of your couch! The world is about
to reveal its microconstituent self, and I was in search,
accordingly, of a painting by Seurat to enter,
all of his atomic confetti! Pardon my error,
I didn't intend to smack through here like an axe-head
from the back of the canvas. And yet, and ye/

Renoir *intended* this disruptive figure,
as a symbol of the unknowableness of existence?
Or, more likely, what emerges from its sticky wall
of pigment is a patron who was x'd-out
for withholding the artist's payment.
"Sister . . . do you sense somebody? Do you *cause*
somebody? When you close your eyes, I hear
a tiresome hum."

/isappeared, eh? Doused. But now
we have returned to one another, and it seems to me
(my pastries in the bakeshop of amour) that our various
sines and coefficients are in harmony again.
Come, join me. You especially, shyly veiling your eyes:
look up! I tell you, we have discovered seventy
chemical elements, Gadolinium just this year!
I tell you that a year from now Monet will begin
the rest-of-his-life seclusion at Giverny, where
his floating, atmospheric compotes of water and light
will serve, in part, to introduce
the field theory and particle physics
of Rothko and of Pollock! Do forgive
my brusque invasion of your snuggery, but
modernity is calling us! Quick,
before I fad/

We can see Renoir in the atelier,
we can sniff the fresh bouquet of oils and turpentine
on the rags. And now he's done for the day.
And on the easel. . . .
A woman, with her eyelids down.
Above her, a visual whisper: "a man."
Maybe he's someone not even born.
Perhaps he's dead. He's dead and yet
he's there, in the painted air. And she
can feel the weight of this close brush.

Second Thoughts

*1862: Dante Gabriel Rossetti buried his young wife Elizabeth Rossetti
with a sheaf of his unpublished poems.*

. . . and then of course the weeping: some demurely, some
flamboyantly. Those elegiac tears, if shed
enough, will alter a face and the person
behind the face. We all know that erosion

is a mighty thing, and even—for example—
the seemingly permanent, hard-black Mississippi banks
undo and slip south. In a sense, the delta
at New Orleans—the land gone silt, and rebuilt—

is the Mississippi's second thought. "My pet,
your wiles have altered my earlier obstinacy,
and the vision of you in your luxury stateroom beckons;
I *shall* join you for your voyage on the Gigantic

—what? oh. Titanic"—is a tragic second thought.
A happy one: when Skyler and I decided to try again
to "save the marriage." Now we're lazing in a pour
of Sunday morning light as orangely voluptuous

as marmalade. A simile's a first thought,
then an equaled next. She slips back into sleep,
and now I'm reading about the night that shady London dandy
Charles Augustus Howell (1869) unshoveled the grave

at Highgate, broke the coffin, and looted her bone breast
of "the book in question, bound in rough gray calf, and with
red edges to the leaves," on eager orders from Rossetti
—who'd had second thoughts in seven years, desiring

to publish now a volume of his verses (1870, *Poems*).
Lizzie's death-stenched pages were saturated
with disinfectant by a medical practitioner "who
is drying them leaf by leaf"—and then they joined the world

of woven radish baskets, bobbered fishing skeins, and god dolls
in their second life as art on a museum wall; a world where
the "conversion pool" saw swimmers step in white robes
from its farther end, reborn to new religion; and the lumbering

land animals said *no*, and gave up legs, and so their legs rolled up
like stored-away and useless rugs inside them, and they returned
to the waters, and birthed and breached in the waters,
and made the waters their orchestral glory,

and spouted out their great Ionic columns of air and water
in the touch of the changing mind of Earth,
that's sunlit at times
and at other times darkened.

Poem Spoken by a Plaque at Scenic View

"We often discover strange-looking structures on insects,
and we can't even imagine *what they're for."*
—Entomologist at the American Museum of Natural History

This one, here, that looks like a melted accordion
under a bozo wig . . . provides an early warning
if even one molecule of useless sprays like Insect-Rid or Bug-Off
gets within a zone approximately the size of the state of Arkansas. And
this one, if you squint and hold your breath you'll see
what seems to be a leopard-spotted fire hydrant
weighed down with Hawaiian leis . . . it's a highly sensitive
node for instantaneous recalibration of flight path
during midair sex. On even the midgiest insect,
dozens of these. Believe me: I'm a scenic view,
and I know my constituent parts
and *their* constituent parts, and so on, down
to the jungle of light
inside a photon (there, of course, even my
awareness stops). In every blacksnake,
any randomly selected wedge the size of an insect
holds this many mysteries. Now times that
by the length of an entire blacksnake. Times that
by the poundage of a bull moose. By a Kodiak bear.
It never stops. The dust motes aren't smooth,
a final Atlas to the Great Crags of the Dust Motes
has yet to be researched. And that photograph
you've stopped at the rail to fussily snap
—it captures me about the way
your driver's license photo captures you.
As always, now that a human being has come within
the frame of reference, this poem is about you,
not about me. And so I think I'll ask you to remember
some earlier episode when . . . let's say that you're a man,

and she's a woman; and the moon-confusing clouds
outside the window, tined with sudden discharged voltage,
are an accurate exterior correlative
of everything that's happened in this room
so far tonight: it's a story of sundering affection,
and of faith, suspicion, triumph,
deep humiliation, pedantry, revulsion, healing . . . all of these
and more, the whole damn pantheon of feelings. I don't know (here,
my awareness stops) which one of them was in you
when you left the house to walk below those clouds and
. . . what? gloat? rage? But you'll remember it:
you'd found a capability that lifted you (or shrunk you)
to a next you. And whatever it was, this thing,
this beetle from under a rock . . . you stopped midstep
at the shock. You didn't know
you had it in you.

Sestina

As There Are Support Groups, There Are Support Words

*The name of his native country pronounced on a distant shore
could not please the ears of a traveller more than hearing
the words "nitrogen," "oxidation of iron" and "hygrometer."*
—Alexander von Humboldt, nineteenth-century scientist-explorer

When visiting a distant (and imponderable) shire,
one longs to hear the cry "Hygrometer!
Fresh hygrometer for sale!" Yes, and when the fair
sex sidles close and coyly murmurs "nitrogen"
into a burly masculine ear, I guarantee you: the translation
is *very* easy. The allurements of a local siren,

whispering the kind of patois a traveler like Lord Byron
favors, never fail to comfort, and to reassure,
evoking pleasant memories of one's own beloved hygrometer
at home, kept fresh in Cosmoline and camphor
and awaiting one's rearrival back in his native xenon and nitrogen.
Without these occasional reminiscences, any translation

from nation to nation, tongue to tongue, becomes a translation
difficult to sustain. I think of my grandmother: "We're not hirin'
today" "Go away" "Dumb Jew"—*her* share
of the language that greeted her here in the land of alien hygrometer
and freedom, where she was only one more funny-skirted for-
eigner yearning to hear a lulling Hungarian nitrogen

hum her to sleep. Eventually, of course, the American nitrogen
sufficed. Her daughter could speak, in free translation,
both uranium and argon; and her granddaughter gigs with Fire 'n
Ice, a skinhead punk-grunge group that performs in sheer
black nighties and clown wigs—she plays mean electric hygrometer
in the first set and then, for a twofer,

(*very* American, that) plays paper-and-comb. Far
out. She's so fluent in various World Wide Webbery that nitrogen
in a thousand different inflections is her birthright, and almost any translation,
mind to mind, gender to gender, is second nature. "I earn
my keep, I party, I sleep" is her motto. Though she's for-
tunate in having a lover who's CEO at Hygrometer,

Potassium, Klein & Wong: it helps to pay the "hygrometer
man" when he knocks at the door. I won't say that they fear
this guy exactly, but he's a major badass nitrogen-
sucking cyberwired ninja-kicking shitheel (or, translation:
call him Sir). It makes one pine for a land where the birds all choir in
sweetly trilling melodies on a flower-scented shore,

and a translation sings all night. Row gen-
tly toward it. The tender forests sigh, and the soft whirr
of the hygrometer promises oxidation of iron.

A Conjugal Beauty

The nineteenth-century eccentric Charles Waterton was a robust, hands-
on traveler. In South America he subdued a cayman alligator by jump-
ing on its back and riding it. "This," as he says, "was an interesting
moment." Explaining that direct approach, John Keay writes, "Other natu-
ralists might have contented themselves with careful observation of the ani-
mals, but Waterton had to come to grips with them—literally."

One cop is up to literally his keester
in a tank of butchered squid—as he says later,
"like a floating combination of rubber and puke."
But he's after a clue, a blue bone button from a sleeve,
and clue retrieval *is* his job: and so it's both heroic
and simply work for a wage that after a while
he holds a breath, then drops in over his head
to feel with his hands along the bottom. His wife
reads stories where the protagonist sits in an armchair
in a private salon, and solves crimes
by the power of thought alone, as if detection were a matter
of logarithms and mental lists—the way that Neptune was discovered,
first by theory and only later confirmed by an actual eye
at an actual lens—the way some people love each other best

apart, and not inside the messy, bushy thick of one another.
In the war of abstract reason versus squeeze-the-muck
experience, each side has its proponents.* A *bokher*
a shatkhan, ken nit zayn: a bachelor
can't be a matchmaker; so goes the Yiddish expression.
Nor is Aristotle, for all of his impeccable logic,
flawless: writhes of maggots *aren't* generated spontaneously
from cheese, or mice asexually from mounds
of dust; and treating such untested "truth" as dogma
for millennia is *not* the way toward any lux or veritas,
bubba. *That* requires some of the sweat and joint-oil
of experiment: Leeuwenhoek cunningly eking out
the goo of sperm and cell-wall from the oviducts
of freshly dissected dogs; or those fanatic zoology students

swallowing tapeworm cysts, then later shitting out
the results to examine. There's a beauty, a truly
conjugal beauty, in having this sleeves-up, pants-down labor
marry—that is, verify—the insights of a blackboard
and a stick of chalk: for example, the voyage Eddington made
to a cocoa plantation on Príncipe Island
off West Equatorial Africa, to observe if there *was*
"curvature of space" around the solar eclipse of May 29,
1919—finally proving the runic equations
of Einstein's general theory of relativity.** But
just as surely, there *must* be a beauty in relying
(out of faith in its authority?) on purest speculation
as it floats above *our* little woes and glees,
untethered by either. Otherwise, why would my friends

* In sixteenth-century Pisa, the proscription against dissection of human corpses in anatomical classes was strictly obeyed; meanwhile, in Padua, laboratory tables were constructed that could secretly be lowered to an underground river, where boats with cadavers unloaded their wares. This is, of course, the dichotomy of Sherlock Holmes, with his hawkish nose tipped down to the blood and the ashes; and his brother Mycroft, puzzling out the same misdeeds through "ratiocination" alone.

** A student, Ilse Rosenthal-Schneider, asked him, "What would you have said if there had been no confirmation?" "I would have to pity our dear Lord," she remembers Einstein telling her, "—the theory is correct."

on the cusp of divorce seek out the advice of this counselor
with *I swear* the babyish celibate-fat of a eunuch
coating his body?—and yet they do. It's part of what
we *mean* by "priest" or "priestess," yes?—uncompromised
by dailiness. In front of him, they open their dirty box:
the bitemarks Z is sporting across her ass like medals;
A's incredibly beery storehouse of lies; the times
their love and hate have made them so close they
were snorkeling, each in the turbid stream of the other's
dream life. "Ah," he says; and promises, from all the signs,
a "breakthrough session" soon. That night, we find him
in his armchair reading Waterton's account, and not the least
persuaded. He'd have done it
differently, if he'd been there, if he straddled the beast.

Canceling Out

In the eleventh century a man in Cologne bought a shipload of anchor
stones, saying, "Sin is a heavy thing, and at the last doom when good and
evil deeds are weighed, those apostles who love me will cast the stones into
the scale of my good deeds and thus save me."
—Richard Erdoes

1

What my Catholic cronies call original sin
alone would require a couple of fully loaded Cadillac Sevilles,
a small Stonehengian circle of bulky 1950s Frigidaires,
the medals and buckles of all of the poo-bahs in Fraternal Lodge 347,
and an extra scatter of tire jacks and foundry molds
as substitution adequate enough.
These are invisible in medieval paintings

of Adam and Eve as they exit the Gates—but
look at how their heads hang
and their backs are bowed, with the junkyard weight
they've just had encoded in humankind's genes.

2

Which sin is counterbalanced by an anvil?
by a dozen anvils? a naval destroyer?
Which requires the impact-weight of a meteorite?
and which is accountable down to the weight
of a single grain of pollen? In the washroom
of Fraternal Lodge 347, a man, a good man, numbly sudses
the whiff of a one-time lapse-in-goodness off his flesh;
but there was drink, and a woman who did an act
with candle wax and a vibrator, and . . . well, anyway . . .
it isn't up to me to say what that might mean
to the wife he betrayed. A backyard rock?
a lesser moon of Jupiter's? a snail

cast in iron they use to keep the daily paper
from being gusted off the stoop? Tonight the paper
was a CIA employee who sold state secrets
and a mother who drowned her three-year-old.
A hod of bricks? a mountain range? the millstones
from a chicken's crop? On infinity's scale,
the planets are only another kind of floating dust.
What penance is fit to a day like today?
What charitable gesture, X,
erases desecration X-1?

3

Pliny says the goby fish—two inches—"will attach itself
to a rudder, it can stall a galley ship of 400 rowers"
. . . a shaky assertion, although it's documented
fact that the Norwegian trawler *Steinholm*,
sixty-two feet long, was capsized, and then sunk, in early 1998
by an enormous catch of netted herring,
which, before the winch could turn, swam bottomward
as one. It seems to me a desperate hope for this
same sudden, overcompensating force—but in the opposite
direction—that uplifts the gazes of Adam and Eve

as they stumble heavily into their mortal future,
in a crackle-surfaced oil dated 1568. Might they
be liberated out of their plight, by some soft-hearted
rescue team of angels? are these near (just inches out of the frame
of the painting), real, and loud as laundered kitchen linen
snapping on the line? and can four hundred angels overcome,
by straining their wings in unison,
the gravity of weeping?

4

Rain is coming; it booms around in its overhead tunnels,
and some of the grimmer clouds up there are already as solid
as I beams. Some of her thoughts have also condensed
to a similar tonnage; some of her memories
seem pile-drivered into her brain.
She hails, then she dozes in, a taxi. . . .
There are two main ways to be "in bed" with someone,
says a chatty *Cosmo*-ripoff magazine she reads to pieces
every month (she needs to "keep up": she's a freelance
ad designer). You can make love with the blazing,
grandstand immolating powers of the sun; or
you can very gently allover nibble each other
like pinpoint stars upon the night. Okay,
but also you can be purchased, you can turn your beam
mechanically off and on like a flashlight. That's
what she's spent three illegal hours at tonight
(an ad designer in this city needs to supplement
her income), and, if she's been a flashlight,
her battery's drained. Pay the cabbie . . . up the stairs . . .
she peeks into her mother's room, where the odor
of chemotherapy burns sickly out of her scalp
like a bad perm. "Hey, you might like one of these,"
her man—her new man, Mr. Ass Tattoo—halloos
from out of the sunroom, thoughtfully offering up
a gin and tonic *so* clear, *so* damn good,
it cancels out its weight in daily circumstance
a zillionfold. He'll want to hear
the story of her evening with the yahoos, and she mutely
raises a tasseled fez that specifies 347
stitched in silver glitter. He slides a chair her way
across the linoleum. "Here. Take a load off your feet."

Astronomy

It dies. And a gazillion years in the future
the sight of its dying reaches Earth.
—Computed in dinosaur years, that's three days
from the brain's death to its being recognized as dead
in the far frontiers of the tail.

Night. A party. "Come out here for a minute."
Dina told me: she'd miscarried. But
her body hadn't registered that yet, it kept
preparing for a birth. And so we sat on the porch
in silence for a while, in the light of that star.

. . . one of whom had apparently died in childbirth;
we found the skeleton of an infant within
her remains.

—*Zawi Hawass, of an archeological dig*

—it was, in its way,
a pietà.

And the pictures in the planetarium gallery
of a star in all the stages of its last progression,
dying—first a "white dwarf," then a "black dwarf,"
then a "black hole," that the composition
cradles in the milkiest arms of the universe.

The Hardy Boys' Detective Handbook (1959)
"Authentic Detective Methods for Solving Mysteries"

1. Taps

Hooligans sapped the shamus and lammed with the swag,
the loot, the kale, the sugar, the bale of simoleons, the do-re-mi
—means studious Joe Hardy is applying himself to Chapter III,
A Dictionary of Underworld Slang. "Oh douse your tonguewag," Frank,
the older Hardy Boy, admonishes, but he's only ribbing (joking).
Joe reveres his older brother, and they both revere their father,
Fenton Hardy, a globally famous private dick (eye). "Now
you two are real sleuths!" he'll say commendingly after
one of their successful novice criminologist forays.
There's a clearly tapshoe'd trail in the mud below this window
where a chambermaid in dishabille was peeped upon. Or
fingerprints, as subtle as the abdominal tracts of bees.
Or fossil tracks that lipstick leaves up the chest of a corpse.
The given wisdom says that crime is the disruption of an ordered world,
as measured in the units we call *clues*. "Wow fellows,"
Chet the pudgy chum exclaims, "you Hardy Boys are whizzes!"
("ace" investigators). Joe *likes* Chet, but Joe goes *total woowoo*
over Chet's elastically agile sis Iola, she who moves with the loose,
wan look of a five-foot-seven length of sexual linguini; also
moves a burning appetite in Joe he never knew he had
and doesn't understand. He doesn't understand how death
(his mother's dead) erases every trace of Who We Are so *thoroughly*;
the plaster casts described in back of Chapter VII can't preserve
the Soul. It's late, he watches the sun like the spiky ball of a mace
and its gold chain along the water. Then it sets
and he goes home. There are, he realizes, mysteries beyond
The Case of the Missing Chinese Vase, or The Adventure of
. . . what did they call it? Maybe the notes are in his brother's closet,
let's see, t-shirts, neckties, shorts, a pair of tapshoe-soled black boots
—of *what*? NO THAT CAN'T B/ *clamp.*

2. Perpvic

One, she loosely based on the faux (yet still expensive) celadon Ming vase
at the foot of the folding Chinese screen in her bedroom. Another,
The Sign of the Yapping Lapdog, on a photo of her ex-mother-in-law
with Pugsie. Altogether, she's done nine insipid titles in this series
of juvie mysteries (under the "house name," Michael Lane,
which is *also* insipid); and while she hates to admit that Nestor's right,
it turns out a control freak *can* occasionally be right: she needs
expanding her limited oeuvre into the lucrative field
of adult crime ("but writing it, not *committing* it," he says for a no-lose
chuckle at parties). A month ago she started her investigative visits
to the Fed pen up in Nyeville, and by now she's past their street names
and their shuck (the "jive," the thick b.s.); she's seen the face
of a five-count ice-pick hit man squeeze itself in uncontrollable tears,
afraid of the dark; she's heard the stories of Rooms by the Hour,
Razors up the Ass, Suck Daddy's Friend. And here
there aren't any masterminds of the kind she used to write about
("I'll-rob-a-different-business-for-every-letter-of-the-alphabet"), no
there's only the broken dancing of Complicity with Ignorance,
and everyone's like the child abuser abused as a child himself,
a perpvic (her neologism): perpetrator and victim in one.
If anything, she feels sweet nostalgia for the world
that "Michael Lane" creates, of undiluted Purity and undiluted Monstrousness.
Some two or three weeks after his release for good behavior,
she met John Yei-Yei Maoke, one of her favorites, on the stoop
of Fun Time Bar-B-Que, and she shared with him
that dream of a world of absolutes. He shook his head:
"Nobody money clean." He lifted a newspaper
off the sidewalk—yesterday's? today's? It didn't matter,
of course, and he jabbed at headlines, Congress this or that.
"It dirty before it leave the mint."

3. Confusion

Joe knows he has "the hot pants" for Iola (erotic attraction).
He's ashamed of both the concept and the phrase; alas, it's 1959
for him, and Bayport High's vocabulary drill will never hold
the word "libido," which at least would lend his puppylust
a scientific dignity. The days pass over Joe like an emery wheel,
by night he feels worn to a rough clay doll of himself. "Hey
bro'," says Frank, "let's have a little chinfest" (talk), as if
he needs to make an admission, or ask some delicate question,
but it's only more detective blab, on How to ID Suspects
("often, the criminal type will show an improperly mended broken nose"),
and Joe looks hard at Frank (a squint? a tic? a scar?), looks even
harder at himself as he squeezes his acne and queasily ponders
the Bible: "Cleanse your hands, ye sinners; and purify your hearts,
ye double minded." Surely he's *that*: he wants Iola
in goddessy airiness on a pedestal of marble, and he wants her
squirming bitch heat under NO HELP NO I/ *clamp.*
He's scared to check the boots below his bed, those taps
could turn up anywhere, from anyone. He thinks he heard
Chet cuss the other day, then wink. "Look, boys, a perfect
tire tread!" says Fenton Hardy, hands still slick with plaster.
"But physical evidence aside, we need to go on to the delicate question
of Chapter XI: Motive." Joe has that, all right: Joe has
a squadhouse lineup's-worth of that, in which *each* face up there
is equally a culprit's. And in English class
at Bayport High, they're doing Whitman's "Crossing Brooklyn Ferry":
"Nor is it you alone who know what it is to be evil,
I am he who knew what it was to be evil,
—Wayward, vain, greedy, shallow, cowardly, malignant. . . ."
Joe reads his assigned few lines aloud as if, under sodium pentathol
(Chapter XII), he's at last confessing the truth.

4. Mirror

She remembers the fragrance released from cut white pine
at her grandfather's lumber business: dry, sweet, and reliable
from plank to plank, year to year. Why can't *her* essence be this
true over time? But after three months with the lifers
up at Nyeville—after a long gray season of wallowing
in the aftereffects of vo(and avo-)cational violence (one guy here
they say provides his empty eye socket for sexual play)—
she flipflops daily, *hourly*, from feeling a kind of lucky
superiority to feeling quite at home among these spirit-fractured
inflicters of damage . . . Alley Stick, Miss Kwikee, Breeze,
and the rest of the incarcerees. She worries: her self-image
is The Nurturer, and yet she's going to flay and quarter
Nestor's susceptible heart: his smugly martinet technique
may be ideal for the local high school English course he commandeers,
but not for love—not, anyway, for *her* love; though to know this,
and to say it to his open hopeful face, are two *completely*
different galaxies, and probably require two completely different
selves of her. The *me* today who looks back from her purse's makeup mirror
is The Butcherer. (It's simply true, the "deacon" who on Sundays
leads the felons in their morning devotional service—soaring
gushingly through sermons on "The Power of Jesus' Spirit"—is
emblazoned with the tattoo'd sentiment *Torture Before You Kill.*)
And finally, this is Nestor's legacy: these visits to the icehouse
(jail). For that, she's thankful (indebted/guilty). She's also
reading the masters of mystery writing. Ross Macdonald's gumshoe
Archer: "I tried smiling to encourage myself. I was a good Joe after all.
Consorter with roughnecks, tarts, hard cases and easy marks;
private eye at the keyhole of illicit bedrooms; informer
to jealousy, rat behind the walls, hired gun to anybody
with fifty dollars a day; but a good Joe after all."

5. Good

The Whispers Motel: Rooms by the Hour is sometimes known to rent rooms
by the fifteen minutes. That kind of place. Let's watch
a couple lick and loll. Let's you and I be rats behind the walls
of room 11; let's appreciate its Mattress-Spring Concerto
for Urgent Organs and Chorus of Moans. But first I want to spy
on the adult future of one Joe Hardy, former junior investigator and now
head family therapist at Community Outreach Services
("shrink")—a different, but not thoroughly dissimilar, search
for clues and resolution. He's one of the luckier ones (if such
conflicted psyches can be designated "lucky" at all): he's
seen the wrestle of Jacob and the angel, understanding it (profoundly)
for the story of a man amoebically splitting and then
contending with his Other. The kids he helps are correct: he's one
cool standup dude. Though as for Frank . . . when he's kicked off the force
for mega-headline graft, it's all a downward-spiral narrative
of bourbon mornings, backseat pussy-sniffing nights,
the trots, the screaming meemies. But I'm talking twenty years
away; for us, just now, the boxy air of room 11 is weighted
with so much human sexual musk it almost qualifies
as a gland. The various self-(or pharmaceutical-)lubricated
mazes, inlets, spindles, jellynooks, and hooklets
of the body are breathily doing their obsessive best. Their
furtive and obsessive best, in this case. After one Big O
and a dwindling drizzle of littler *o*'s in lowercase, they laze around
in one another's spraddled legs and suck the rankish sugar glaze
off one another's skin. Their hour's nearly up; their spent libido,
down. The workday plaster from his hands is still a ladder
up the mussed pleats of her cheerleader skirt. Iola says,
"Oh baby you were goooood," and Fenton Hardy grunts, zips up,
and slips inside his kick-ass tapshoe-soled black boots.

Glass

*Sitting in the audience of the anatomy lesson Rembrandt painted would
have been "Caspar Barleus, a local poet and intellectual and neurotic with
an odd relationship to his own body, a man who was afraid to sit down
because he might shatter his buttocks, which he said were made of glass"*
(Charles L. Mee Jr.).

—which would have made enemas challenging.
And the seventeenth century "might be called," as William Heckscher says
in his study of Rembrandt, "the Age of the Enema." In one year,
Louis XIII was administered two hundred and fifteen. Nicolaas Tulp,
Rembrandt's friend/physician, ordered a regimen of enemas
for the artist during that pitiful nine months when he believed
his bones were softening and "might easily buckle
like wax"—this also being the great Age of Melancholia;
any man or woman of genius, any genius-wannabe,
succumbed to this condition, and provided it (as Rembrandt
with the melting of his skeleton) an individualized,
credentialing emblem. Here, the "cradle dresses"
sewn for the Countess of Fytchling-Griswold, thirty-two, who
over one year retrogressed to infancy (complete with wet nurse).
Here, the padlock Samuel Johnson's confidante and keeper
Mrs. Thrale used, to threaten his more rabid antisocial spasms
into something milder. If it's true, what the neurocartologists
claim—the brain is the densest field of interconnection
in the cosmos—then these symbols of personal suffering say
a pain can be mapped out to coincide with the whole of the universe.

———————

On July 10, 1997, my friend Devin Neddicks stepped out
onto the window ledge of the seventeenth floor of the Morrison Building.
Far below, the greenhouse of a garden display
was barely a glint the size of a wadded cellophane wrapper
fracturing light on its panes. For a full year after
the divorce, he'd been a little . . . *strange;* we nicknamed him
El Nutto. Another century might have leeched him, might have
carriaged him away to a spa; instead, in ours, the pseudo-calm of choice
was pharmaceutical. To every age, its own
concocted metaphors of neediness; its own concocted remedies.
("Angels" = "UFOs," etc.) Rembrandt's lassitude was wax;
for Devin, nadir'd out from his blowsy and manic shenanigans,
it was Iron 56 or, as he put it to me, "the most
inert natural substance known." *Huh?* I said, and he
rephrased it in Albertese: "Atomic zilch." That was early
April. On the morning of July 11, I visited the scene.
Behind the yellow police tape, nothing had been cleaned,
and the traces of greenhouse splinters and human blood
—so fine in places it might have been a mist—took up
a full square block: the fossil of an agony that originally
fit inside a seed in Devin Neddicks's mind.

———————————

In Rembrandt's *The Anatomy Lesson of Dr. Tulp*, we see the first
dissection cut—the left arm of the corpse is stripped of skin—
already leads us to a shadowy hollow so far back
amid the mysterious cave twists of the body, it may *not*
be body, but some plane where the living "me" gets formed.
The cadaver, a pale wave the tint of soured milk, is/was
an Aris Kindt from Leyden, brawler, thief, attempted killer:
is the engine of his failed self (or by extension, *anybody's*
self) inside this maze of human webbery and tubers
somewhere? That's a question possible to force
upon a purely anatomical proceeding in year 1632,
and Tulp undoes the forearm's muscles with
not only deft precision,* but a pride in the importance
of his diagnostic art. In the audience (standing,
of course) is Caspar Barleus, who I imagine
must be thinking how efficient *he* would be if laid there
for inspection, whose cold flesh would hold a window.
"I would be the famous case in which . . ."—and Tulp is demonstrating
how a flex *here* is a reflex *there*—". . . the problem
and the lens of its discovery are one."

----

* He also authored a description of the Chinese tea ceremony.

And one believed a horn grew from his head, "to the extent
that he must raise in height his doorways."
One believed that birds stole human breath to fuel their flying;
she would faint away on public streets if birds were in the trees.
There are no stories starring legendary figures—only
legends. For the rest of us, the stories of our woes are sometimes
so small that they masquerade as everyday contentment. Listen:
over their bed, Devin and Allie had long ago positioned
a print of *The Jewish Bride*; as Charles L. Mee Jr. says,
"The couple seem to appear in a dream or a vision . . . and
the moment is one of the purest love, the only such moment
Rembrandt ever painted." Where their hands touch on her breast,
they blend, in a resonant mutuality. So when one day
—as the tale is told in my vale of compadres—Allie
grabbed the picture off one wall and smashed it at another
in a rage, at first we couldn't believe it. But there
was the crack, a jagged split that made a joke
of the UV-protective coating and the goldspatter scrollwork frame.
And as for Devin . . . you know. It wasn't only the marriage;
that was also the moment his reason shattered.

The Geese

*In the evening, at the suggestion of Orpheus, they beached the ship at
Samothrace, the island of Electra daughter of Atlas. He wished them, by
a holy initiation, to learn something of the secret rites, and so sail on with
greater confidence across the formidable sea. Of the rites I say no more,
pausing only to salute the isle itself and the Powers that dwell on it, to whom
belong the mysteries of which we must not sing.*
—Jason and the Argonauts,
   Apollonius of Rhodes (translated by E. V. Rieu)

On a brittle winter afternoon in Moscow, the American,
Houdini, was professionally stripped and searched, then
manacled, and then locked in an eyesore "work camp transport carriage,"
at the Butirskaya Prison, "the strongest and oldest
of the Russian prisons." He freed himself
in twenty-eight minutes—chattering and violet-lipped
before the gathered wardens; and
victorious. The only sound for fifteen endless seconds
was a V of black geese overhead; but then Houdini
clowned one opened leg-cuff onto his head, for a crown,
and the knot of frowning officials sent their cheer out
like a single round of goblets thrown
to break against the hard air. How he did it? . . .
is a secret; is a trick, but is a pineal eye
of a trick, deep-set in the center of him.
We'll *never* know.
In fact that afternoon, in its entirety,
is woven out of secrets. That Houdini was a Jew,
in Russia, in 1903, recklessly
inaugurating four triumphant months
of touring cities where the populace was known to disembowel a Jew
and make him stare as street pigs ate his own unrolled
intestine to its root . . . *that* was a tremulous secret.
The prison itself?—in 1950, Stalin ordered "factories
erected around it, to block it from view.

It's not even listed on Moscow maps, although
it's in the very heart of that city." And who knows *what* thoughts
irrupted like sour rosettes, or flowered
as lavishly as magnolias,
in the minds of that fortress's prisoners
when they peered out from their cells' barred slits
to witness the foreigner exit his iron shackles
with the ease (this is the way they would see it)
of smoke? Who knows what other selves are locked away
in *anybody's* brain stem? The most public
and most obvious occurrence in this scene
might be those sky-high geese I introduced:
they're honking, loud and declarative,
like an advertisement for freedom.

———————————

When my Great-Auntie Yetta eluded the baying Jew-hounds of the tsar
and one night slipped across the border . . . she became Yvette,
and traveled as that flouncy incognito-her
for three years with a troupe of rural "actresses,"
who were tacitly granted a shabby kind of security
against the routine ID checks
of state police: the services they offered
after-hours kept them separate from whatever charge
of tainted Hebrew lineage might otherwise apply. "Yes, so?
To live, I kiss these men," is how she put it (I was only ten).
"I maked them feel happy from my company"—who until then
had never held a grown man's hand unchaperoned. "But
more, I shouldn't say." Which is a credo
that Houdini understood: his own escapes
have left their physical accoutrements behind
(the shackles, still preserved
in one of the towers of Butirskaya Prison),
but the *how* of them is mute; the oaths of silence
his assistants and constructioneers were bound by
were, it turns out, more restricting
than the locks and knots and coffins of his shows.
Houdini's water-torture cell is on display in the museum
of historically important magic apparatus

stored now in the megamillion-dollar home of celebrity
conjuror David Copperfield—a building camouflaged
as the B. S. Kotkin Bras & Girdles Mail Order Division.
"It's very deceptive." O we must not sing of the mysteries,
of the bird that lives in the flower, of the flower
that lives in the empty sleeve, o we must not sing
of the pulse in the body that wants more
than its single human lifetime. I suppose
one part of the joke is that the bra and the girdle *do*,
in their own schoolboy-humor manner, both conceal
and announce our pleasure's private holy places.
(Also "holey": more of that schoolboy humor.) I remember
laboring the bra off—finally!—Edith Thelma Szelmann, and
the bobbing spill of breastflesh that surprised her
just as much as it did me, we were so new at this
—so young, we thought that all we'd ever ask for from a lover
was bare skin. It was autumn. The park was a motionless ocean
of amber leaves. We rolled through these, we burrowed thick in them
and nipped and licked, with the tang of vegetable rot
our aphrodisiac. And overhead: those migrating geese,
an arrow to someplace unknowable.

————————

"The smallest guitar in the world is about the size
of a human blood cell, with the width of around one-twentieth
that of a human hair. . . ." *O we must not sing*
". . . It was sculpted from a layer of crystalline silicon
on an oxide substrate using a beam of electrons. . . ."
O we must not, o we can not ". . . You could strum
this guitar with the tip of a single atom, but
the sound would be at frequencies inaudible to the human ear."
O we must not sing, o we can not sing,
the music of the mysteries.
And the women can't intone the prayers of the men
in the orthodox synagogue. And the men can't enter
the "cycle hut" of the women in the N'zele tribe.
And then she moaned—there were no words.
And the gods come forth, in radiance so absolute
they can't be seen. And the penitent flaps ecstatically

on the sawdust floor, and chatters speech
they used in Eden, but not in our vale of suffering.
And then she moaned, in untranslatable pleasure
—although I was there, I wasn't on *her* side of "there."
O *we must not sing.* And if the women *do*
hijack the prayers of the men, then they will come to know
the spleen and the contumely of the Lord, for He will lay asunder
that congregation of black-babushka'd deviants like bowling pins,
for the word of His commandment is inviolable. And if the men
do enter, and do so profane, the "cycle hut" of the moon
and the menstrual ritual; and if the child *does* self-countermand
the parents' stricture, if the five-year-old does enter
the forbidden room, and sees the mother astraddle the father,
rapt in their unfathomable duet; and if the lost WAC
in the wrong wing of the underground construction *does*
unseal the vault, and looks in, at the saucerthing,
the horribly half-familiar and yet completely othergalactic being
hidden there . . . O *we must not sing*
divulgingly of the mysteries. The priestess in the cave-mouth
keeps such secrets of the Heavens and their deep,
bedarkened counterparts!—the incense smoke
that roils from the brazier cup and wreathes her
is a secret smoke; her snake-dance is a secret,
sacred, oracular dance.
And then did I taste of the sanctum-place
between her legs, her personal salt; and she,
her taste of me. She did moan. We did turn
in the leaves, like a motor. Then it was done, and it wasn't
enough, the singing is never enough, it calls us
further, and truer, and endlessly into its ultra-puzzle
every time. We want the neutron
and the proton and the unguessabletron, and beyond.
We must not talk of this in our everyday speech,
in breath spent from our everyday lungs.
We let the fall breeze cool our skin;
and stared at the skies "where [Galway Kinnell says] geese
cross at twilight, honking
in tongues."

————————

The way that magic works is
by diversion: nerdy pratfall,
limber-lengthed assistant's spotlit legs,
symphonic calliope oompah-pah
. . . while underneath, some modest thing the size of a thimble
nimbly sews away. But more, I shouldn't say.
HOUDINI TAKES MAGIC SECRETS TO HIS GRAVE
(Oct. 31, 1926, the *New York Sun*).
The Needle Swallowing Trick.
The Nest of Boxes.
Bullet Catching.
De Kolta's Marvellous Cube.
The Magic Rose Bush.
Walking Through a Brick Wall.
Vanishing Elephant.
But mostly of course his legacy is matchless
"escapeology" to the point of, seemingly, miracle:
The Mirror Cuff Escape, The Straitjacket Escape,
The Suspended Straitjacket Escape, Nude Jail Cell Escape,
The Underwater Handcuff Release, The Mailbag Escape,
The Milk Can Escape, The Chinese Coffin Escape . . . at death
his body, finally, must have looked like one more
sloughed entrapment. Once I saw
a stage magician's spangled padlocks in a pawnshop case;
across the floor, a populous display of half-price wedding rings.
So many ways of slipping from restraint. I stopped
to visit Yetta's grave on a malicious autumn day
so chill the breath was like a gray silk scarf.
I told her I was divorced. I said
I'd published a book. I asked her what it means
that a life is a diary
nobody opens and reads completely. And if silence
is ever an answer, she was movingly profound.
She asked me questions back—in silence. Then she lectured me
—in silence. Only the sky was loud, was
. . . well, it's tempting to give you more lines about geese.
But the point is, this was never about
the geese to begin with.

———————

This is about how I can't tell you
what this is about. And yet, for closure's sake,
I'll say it in avian imagery:
An old friend told me she was into the Audubon Society now.
"Hummingbirds migrate across the country
too, although we never see it happening"
—a thread in the lining.

Transplanting

Jessie watched me drive away. I turned off Camino at the first corner, U-turned and parked a hundred feet up the side street, ready to go north or south. The street was shadowed by broad-leaved trees whose names I didn't know, and there were children playing in the twilight.
—Ross Macdonald's detective hero, Lew Archer,
   on the trail of a suspect

1. Sweet William

Hours pass.
A man sits in a dark car on a dark street
—and he might be, as we put it, in the dark

about distinguishing an elm from a catalpa,
though he does know how to ID a schmuck in a lineup,
and he won't be thrown from the track of a foreign shoe sole
through the grubbiest way stations of a druggie's night,
he's literate in this patois,
he's read the food in puke to map a suspect's recent past.
And whether a plant might be an annual or a perennial . . .

he's sorry, but he's not the only reader
to encounter *wainscot,*
fo'c'sle, newel, fetlock, plinth, portcullis,
harrier, reticule, ottoman, negus,
shrug, then keep on reading,
trusting the gist of the action. And
for him, the rows of street trees are peripheral soft-focus

—his adventures in the foul or ritzed-up
pissholes of this world, a sharper
foreground resolution. Unable
even to provide the tidy grade-school labels for something
so essentially close as the great arterial tree
his body breathes by, still
he thinks that he could recognize his suspect's breath
by now, by an individual cheesy fetor.
Yet it's simpler this time:
a man leaves Jessie's apartment, and our hero
follows, car and car, a deceptively laggard two blocks back,
confident in every countermove that matches schmucko's moves.
And Jessie

is oblivious to all of this. As soon as he leaves,
she fusses, in the night air,
at the window box of flowers he brought her yesterday
—named after him, he joked. Already
she's studied up assiduously on soil acidity,
supplements, sun levels—surely
loving these shell-pink flowers that are synonymous
with the man she loves. (Her research will lead her
to study photosynthesis, and the hungry chemical links
of the "spongey palisade layer"; eventually
she'll become an important botanist—but
that's a future life, outside the boundaries
of this poem.) What she does *not* know
is that Billy traffics crack inside The 8-Ball
after closing every Friday. Schmucko.
That, her otherwise fertile heart
could never imagine, and wouldn't believe;
that fact her computer ("Omniscia," as she calls it)
could never download for her.

2. Slow Scroll

broughams, barouches, curricles
—I've asked my wife to research *lung diseases*
on the Web (*I'm* still a willing technoluddite);
and because the site she finds begins its story with *consumption,*
that Victorian idea, and with a sketch of Victorian life,
the names of these very Victorian vehicles fill the screen,
and conjure . . . nothing really, carriages
that blur past through the thickness
of 150 intervening years.
the chaise-and-four, the landau . . .
The *physician* will arrive in a *gig.*
Or maybe (they drew a rigid distinction)
the *surgeon,* if bodily contact were required
—applying leeches, sawing into a gangrened leg.
Or if the patient were of the poor, then the *apothecary*
dispensed advice along with the *elixirs.* And what
did the dying *consumptive* spatter out of his chest?
Well, some things never change:
"Tom has spit a leetle blood this afternoon,"
writes Keats of his brother in 1818,
handily supplying a unit of measurement
that was just as true in 1996, when finally
the nicotine gardened my mother's lungs
and used them up completely
for the sake of its sour brown flowers.

———————————

berlin, charabanc, cabriolet, hackney, phaeton, victoria
—carriages. *So* much has altered, the language itself
betrays us. 1833: *snob* means
the opposite. *Pure* is another word
for dogshit. 1833: it's only four years since
the first true horse-drawn public bus—the *omnibus*—
begins its route; the London bobbies
won't exist for six more years;
the surgeons still employ the *resurrectionist*
(two guineas per cadaver) for their fresh supply
of practice bodies. Time between that vanished world and ours
can seem equivalent to the space between the Earth and Mars.
So—all the more amazing, then,
to realize the fully ripened zeitgeist of millennium 2000
first gets seeded in the ground
of 1833,
        as Charles Babbage,
abetted by Byron's daughter Ada, the Countess of Lovelace,
starts his lifelong labor on a machine that will automatically calculate
tables of tides, with a printer, and memory storage,
what the Countess calls the *Analytical Engine*, and what we call
a computer (a computer of *its* era:
run on steam). So that
the infobaggage we pack can finally be as large
as "air" is large, as numerous as atoms.
So that, in a poem I'm writing, Jessie
loses herself in a downloaded list of flora
common to Victorian fiction: *whortleberry*
("also called *bilberry*"), *woodbine, burdock,* etc.
So that, in the life I'm living, a wife looks up
from her humming screen and asks me do I know
that there's a lung disease called
pneumonoultramicroscopicsilicovolcanoconiosis?

———————————

A man I know is dying.
Emphysema. In another year, the supplemental
canisters won't be enough—his own
lung-lace inside him will fail completely.
Except: he's risen to the top of the priority list
in "sector seven." *That's* why I've requested this
slow scroll through all of *lung diseases*: I want to know
the odds, the pain, the white lies,
under *transplant.*
                              Now a dead man's lung
is going to be grafted into his laboring body.
An alien saint in his niche.
A panel out of an alien diptych.
Ah, but no poeticism can hold
the horror and the hope of this.
A dead man's lung. (Or a woman's?
—someone who, one time, in a bar, on a beach,
might have taken his breath away.)

". . . an attack of spitting of blood,"
wrote Keats, of his own condition, in 1820.
Severn says of Keats, on December 14,
"a Cough seized him, and he vomited
near two Cup-fulls of blood."
My friend has experienced this,
a leetle. My friend, with his thread
of entering-the-21st-century's-medical-science
optimism, still understands
that for all of the differences—*tilbury,*
growler, hansom, trap—
the *hearse* is a carriage

we and Keats will always know in common.

3. The Intermarriage

Midnight. Jessie
tends to her plants the way,
an hour earlier, she tended to her man,
and now they substitute for him.
She studies each leaf with the empathy
a palm reader brings to an open hand.
Traveling in its veins . . .
and in the microscopic mysteries of the stomata . . .
and in the green nave where the sunlight
transubstantiates to sugar. . . .
How inseparably she loves her man: the way,
on her block, there's simply no telling
where one bough ends and another begins.

———————

My friend is a student of literature; he tells me
when he thinks of his upcoming wedding
of chest and lung, he also thinks
—can't help *but* think—of Yeats's sonnet "Leda and the Swan."
Out of hundreds of possible questions one could ask
about the penetration of flesh by animal/godhood,
Yeats's is: "did she put on his knowledge,"
did it transmit fully, through the intermarriage
of physical systems?
There is no provable answer, but

in the days that followed her heart-lung transplant operation
at Yale–New Haven Hospital in 1988, "Claire Sylvia,
47-year-old dance instructor from Queens, New York,
found she was craving new, strange things: green peppers,
chicken nuggets, beer." Her favorite color switched
from red to green. She was tempted to whistle at miniskirted women.
She dreamed repeatedly of a young man
named Tim L.—"in one dream, kissed him,
sucking his body into her own." *You guessed it*:
after luck and detectiving, she discovered her donor
had been an eighteen-year-old man, Tim Lamirande,
whose family said he loved beer, that his favorite color
was green, that "when he crashed into a tree without a helmet,
he had been carrying a box of chicken nuggets." *

Surely we've all been lost inside a larger,
greater *something* than ourselves.
I won't wax prolix now on either religion or sex,
I won't elaborate my vision of the internetted
hive-mind of the rushin'-at-ya future.
I'm just going to remember when I watched a deer
—a giant, candelabrum-antlered buck—at day's end
leap into the last few burning seconds
of the setting sun, and disappear
along with it, as completely
as if in suttee.

* "American surgeon Bruno Cortis has studied more than 300 transplant patients and has found that
nearly 60 per cent have strong post-operative memories that are not their own. 'The memories came
from donors in 90% of these cases,' he claimed" (*Fortean Times*, July 1997). As Keats says in a letter:
"They interassimulate."

4. Hot Links

And at thirty-six, Ada, Countess of Lovelace, will die
of cancer-pain *so* violent
the servants will need to pad her room in mattresses.
And Charles Babbage will die at eighty, his great Machine
a dream still—though a viable dream, awaiting
the right technology. (His brain, to this day, is on display
in two jars—one per hemisphere—in the Hunterian Museum.)
And time will pass, and links will reveal themselves.
And human generations will beget
new generations of old ideas.
And ENIAC will be brought forth—"become," the texts say,
"operational"—in 1946: one hundred feet
by ten by three deep, and with *eighteen thousand* vacuum tubes:
at thirty tons, a city in itself,
of streets of circuitry and sleepless calculation.
And in 1998 I'll watch my wife call *emphysema*
to the screen of a machine
about the size of a slice of toast.
And it will contain the engine "search,"
and it will seek until it finds,
and we will know . . . at last . . . now . . . *everything*,
it will be electro-silo'd away, and awaiting
electro-retrieval, and nothing,
nothing will be lost to us—the way, for example,
taxes came to discriminate against oxcarts
in fifth-century Arab territories, camel trade
reigned totally, the cart-roads fell to disrepair,
and for over a thousand years the word
for a wheeled vehicle vanished
from the Arab language—not *us*, now,
so busy developing gills with which to breathe
in the electro-sea of facts,
we will know everything; except, perhaps,
the usual: God, ourselves, the future, etc.
Jessie laptops

stats on nitrates from a site called SoilServe.
She doesn't know she'll be
the Oscar Röttgelbb Botany Researcher of the Year, one year
a decade after all of this is over.
And she doesn't know what's goin' down,
what's it, what's what, what's happnin,
in the reefered air of party houses just ten miles distant,
through the after-midnight inkiness.
Let's leave her here, like this. Let's drive away.
Let's leave her repotting and singing under her breath.
We have a dark appointment
with another world's proficiencies.

It used to be strictly a pool room,
though a few of the girls ambitiously marketed
pussy on the side, and a few of the high-fives always managed
to exchange a C for a packet of midgrade toot.
But mostly, Bobby's Ballz was where you went
for serious pockets; still is,
but when Nip-Me added her barbecue wagon out back,
it changed to Bobby Cue, and the hot links
now are an equal attraction, though no one better
greasy up the table felt, or else. Some older members
of the community remember it as The 8-Ball.
Six or seven street chicks simply call it home.
It's Friday night

and the Saturday morning paper, short
of any hoo-ha national scandal, will be full of this,
though no one even suspects it's about to occur.
(Well . . . you and I do, from our vantage point
outside of the poem.) And none of the regulars here
could name the commonest variety of tulip, or talk
for fifteen seconds straight about the cambium layer.
None of them knows Keats said this: "So you
are determined to be my mortal foe—draw a Sword
at me, and I will forgive—Put a Bullet in my Brain,
and I will shake it out as a dewdrop from a Lion's Mane. . . .
Men should bear with each other—The best of Men
have but a portion of good in them." But each of these

habituees of the pool hall has his own candescent passions
—whatever they are—and his own expertise.
For instance, Mr. Schmucko has been trailed for all of these lines,
all of these pages, by a man for whom
the spoor of human knavery is an obvious text.
These two confront each other . . . / then a gun
reshapes the noises of the room . . . / a siren . . . / very sudden
emptying of the room . . . / a corpse. . . . Sunday morning,

my friend gets his new lung.
A week goes by, and the breathing is seamless.
He's the afterlife
a lung is resurrected into,
perfectly. And the donor is supposed to remain
a secret, but my friend's wife is so thankful,
so insistent, that a nurse is persuaded at least to reveal
a first name. All that day, my friend's wife
walks around with gratitude for this man's timely dying
like a tiny lozenge of honey on her tongue. This dear, sweet
savior of her husband, this sweet William.

The Lives of Gods and Armoires

A Continuum

Saint Isidore (born c. 560 A.D.) wrote, according to the Fortean Times, *"a 20-volume work encapsulating all the learning of the time, from theology to furniture."*

1.

Well I went went went to heaven, baby baby
—There was light in my head
(de DOOP, ba, de DOOP, ba, de DOOP de DOOP)
I say there was glory in my brain and in my breath
And in my heart, oh but instead
(de DOOP, ba, de DOOP, ba, de DOOP de DOOP)
You know I just wanted your fine bodyyyyyzoop!
Layin' by me in our bed
(de DOOP de DOOP de DOOP, ba, de DOOP de DOOP)

Well I went to the world of abstractions, baby baby
—I could float in the sky
(de DOOP, ba, de DOOP, ba, de DOOP de DOOP)
I say I was there with Truth and the Infinite,
With Thought, and with the Soul, and I could fly
(de DOOP, ba, de DOOP, ba, de DOOP de DOOP)
But I just wanted to be in bed with you,
Lovin' in J-e-r-s-e-y!
(de DOOP de DOOP de DOOP, ba, de DOOP de DOOP)

2.

Once you have a chair

you also have a theoretical chair,
an ideal chair, a spirit chair,
afloat at the top of the air,
a chair that can't be proved.
Would you sit in it? Would you

sit in it over the gorge a mile deep?
A chair that requires faith.

———————

It's like the word and its referent:
stone and "stone," for example.
Even "example." This
is a codependency we've made of them,
the concept and its anchoring thing.
They need each other
the way that "god" is there

in the icon; there by the chrismal;
there at the altar, nostrils flared,
inhaling our part of the contract.

———————

In the sky, what Plato said
are Forms. And they precede
our world. I suppose a cloud is a Form

for rain that cleans and scums and sinks inside
our own imperfect dailiness.
We might imagine thunder
and the sear of lightning, great celestial fracas,
as if something's being made
up there. A long night,
wet and violent. Then it's morning,
and quiet: we walk out to the fields

and in that great expanse,
where none had been before, from out of nowhere:
a chair.

3.

One tick—one putz's little sizzle of hate—
and the devotion of over seven thousand years is turned
to char and splinters. Who *did* bomb
the synagogue? That's the immediate question,
once it's ascertained no one was trapped inside,
thank God. You see?—"thank God." It isn't very long
before the second question: Does one's access to a god
disappear when the structures of that access disappear,
the *bimah*, the Ark that holds the Torah scrolls, etc.?
Well of course not; do we think that prayer
and revelation require wires, e-screens, sculpted columns?
No. And yet . . . the juju
is the otherworldly spell—the potent,
disincarnate Mystery itself—*and*
is the talismanic hank of straw and tail-hair and grave-clay
that the disincarnate lives in. There were rabbis
in our neighborhood as traumatized as any
of the members of the congregation—traumatized
and weak—who in the aftermath denied a possibility
of prayer (or anyway of *efficacious* prayer)
without the shaping space of an enclosure and its furnishings
to reinforce the frail, limping singsong of the human voice.
Let's say a woman's wandering around that sad debris
before the cleanup crew arrives . . . as if she needs to see
how total this destruction is—to bend, and touch
its edges—to believe
in anger capable of abnegating this much
of a city block; *it fit inside somebody's heart!*
Is there a physics somewhere that makes sense of this disaster?
Quantum Fester Theory 101. She has the monstrous urge
to slip her sandals off and run
barefoot across this plain of glass and shrapnel,
maybe *that* would make the lesson clear:
this chaos was *intended* to hurt. She wants to lift
a handful of these glass shards and these splays of wooden splinters
to her nipples, which are intensely alive now
—why? *is she crazy?* (maybe, the situation
is crazy), why? to ruin her own flesh
in an empathy with these—the *kiddush* goblets,

and the cantor's cedar lectern, and the rest—that have been ruined
but have no way to cry their suffering? Whatever
easy spin we give these fantasies of hers,
the bottom line is: they're intensified displays of what
would otherwise be normal, steady stewardship
of objects where her god lives: a *megillah* case,
the intricate *aron hakódesh* with its seraphim in bas-relief,
the chests in which the *siddúrim* are stored. Now, is the god
an equally viable presence in the rubble of these?
Or is it like Jeremy?—he was in her arms, all
eighteen years (plus seven months
of tumor-rampant hell) when, in a silent beat of time,
his waxy, bubbled breathing stopped
forever: something—*who knows what, but something*—
that had been in him, and *was* the "him" of him, was gone,
and what remained was just a stick of manikin.
She tries to puzzle out the linkage: God is holy:
so the word of God is holy: so the book (we'll say
the bench on which the word of God abides until called forth)
is holy: . . . is it? is the book *as object* holy? isn't that
idolatry? Yes, but when they close the book
they frankly kiss its cover. She remembers once when Jeremy was six
and they were in Georgia during flood time, they
were standing on a bank and watching couches,
loveseats, beds, the whole lost stock of someone's luckless
small-town furniture store go bobbing down the water. "Look,
Mommy," he pointed, "those chairs are carrying the river!"

4. A Song about Colonial Times

—also chayer, chaier, chaire, cheere, cheyre.
Not that the wealth of variant spellings
meant that their dwellings
were rich in these: most were spare-

ly furnished, "men and women
using stools or a bench ordinarily";
in the days of the Massachusetts Bay Colony,
after all, "chairs were not common

even in England." They look so serious
and practical, symbols of pi-
ety made of sturdy wainscot oak. To the eye
of the twenty-first century, even the most "luxurious"

have the hard lines of severe and
puritanical philosophy. And a large
percent of chairs for which we recognize the orig-
inal owners *were* used by the officially reverend:

Roger Williams, who, in a letter a
congregant wrote, was called "a godly minister"; Ezekiel
Rogers, reverend and owner of "ten chares"; Will-
iam Penn, our seminal Quaker; etc.

It's easy to imagine them sitting in wonder
and religious zeal so long, so lost, in such a hu-
man/furnishing symbiosis, that when they *do*
at last stand up, it might seem, in the chair's under-

standing, to be a kind of astral projection:
its sentience floating away. And speak-
ing of the Reverend Ezek-
iel Rogers . . . we must add that his selection

of "chares" was accompanied by "quishings" (that
is, cushions); in upholstery, there were velvet, satin,
plush, silk, serge, "and even sealskin"
chairs, *all* idea of comfort not

being completely disregarded as the century went
onward. Still, their sense of lush decor
was never that of the Roman emperor
Elagabalus, who "deposited his excrement

in pots of gold." No, not this breed; they
sat on wood the way they walked *among* the woods
of their new home, bonding with its amplitudes
and promise through the most everyday

of their objects: "And betimes I am aware
how the Eternal and the hosts of Heavn
do Speake or flowr or rattel me even
throgh a milking stoole, or my plain cheayr."

5.

Also, in 1673, the goodwife Faithine Winterthorpe, who fell asleep while laboring in the cider grove, was visited by an incubus, and it had its lickerish way with her, and despoiled her. And also, Thomas Satterfall, of the carpentry family Satterfalls, who lived with his father Matthias and sister Elizabeth in the house attached to the stables out at Mercy Hill . . . was attacked in June by a succubus as he slept, which is a fact, because his father and sister heard him cry in alarm, and because the Devil is ever awake and in command of invisible millions, and because his nightshirt evidenced the stain of that impure nocturnal encounter. And these are not the only instances, the histories are replete with carnal linkings in which one of the parties shows no literal carnalhood at all, but is a spirit.

Of the line between these disembodied visitors and the real human bodies with which they have sexual congress—whether this line is imaginary or actual, whether it's permeable or resistant—much has been written in annals theological, psychological, sociological. What's the line between the firing neuron and the thought to which it contributes? What's the line between the mind and the brain? Can we say that the brain is furniture for the mind? That words are furniture for meaning? Surely myth is the table on which a culture's various explanations rest.

A culture/epoch/zeitgeist *is* its furniture (and is also its dominant architecture); so are the people belonging to that culture/epoch/zeitgeist. It's a Weimar Republic man in a Weimar Republic time in a Weimar Republic chair; it's my friend Cole in the inflatable, transparent lime-green "Lounge-Around" that he bought one day as an afterthought on the e-shop site for Sidekix. (In her book *The Artificial Kingdom*, Celeste Olalquiaga refers to Walter Benjamin's concept of the "furnished man": exterior physicality—of *his own, specific, daily repeated* exterior world—"presents itself to his touch and ends up forming figures inside him.")

"The Wassily armchair, designed by Marcel Breuer in 1925–26 . . . is a structure of bent, chromed-metal tubing . . . recall[ing] a bicycle frame" (Witold Rybczynski); meanwhile, the honored parents in *Filial Piety* (China, 1100s, watercolor) easily sit, their legs crossed, on a rug. Bauhaus. Baroque. The cluttery, bric-a-bracked front parlors of Holmes's Victorian London: shells and teacups and paperweights and robins' eggs and framed hair from the family's dead and china cats and taxidermied weasels in their thick, glass-front armoire. Whatever "semen" tells us, "jism" says another thing. Language is the furniture in which a sensibility arranges and comports itself.

The desk in the abbess's office is so plain, with such *intensity* of plainness, that it asks to be not only a mnemonic of her life's renunciations, but (against all hopes of modesty) an honorific one. And then again, as Jean-Luc Hennig claims, Toulouse-Lautrec "is said to have painted 'fleshy, common tarts on red sofas.'"

And what did the Puritan bed of Thomas Satterfall say, and was its public dis-course any different from the nightmare things that whispered in the dark maze at the back of his mind? I don't know. But I know what I see in this statue of an Etruscan couple reclining together—two relaxed, contented parallel lines—atop a couch that's evidently been designed with just such pleasant postcoital mutu-ality in mind. Among its many lovely implications, this: *there might be hope for all of us.*

6.

The denizens of heaven have no bodies,
unless a "body" of light is a body. I say it isn't.
They're greater than human beings, of course;
yet less than vapor on a window,
less than trails of neutrinos. They're
the answer to the question: Void divided by Holiness equals?
Nothing inferior to this is allowed to stand before God.
And they *do* stand, or they circle
like rosy zeppelins, in medieval paintings: necessary
artistic convention has given these ethereals a physical form.
And even God, who isn't "who" in any way
we'd understand that word . . . yes, even God,
the More-than-the-Universe . . . He sits on a throne,
with all that implies: stature, image, buttocks.

———————

God, in fact (if we can accept the ancient Jewish apocalypse story
The Ethiopic Book of Enoch as fact),
is far more human in appearance
than his radiant minions: "angels," I. P. Couliano says
in his study of "otherworldly journeys," "have no joints.
Only God can sit and the angels cannot." I used to visit
a basement lounge—the kind out near the shanties,
though the ritz and the cognoscenti were in attendance—and here
we all stood, we were grateful to be standing there,
to be there but also transported *from* there at the same time,
as the jazz pianist T-bone Rogers sat at his keys
with an easy, bluesy mastery of the room. I suppose
notation is a furniture for music. And I *know*
the women there were a sumptuous furniture for my eyes.

———————

As these painters have given Him "arms" and "legs,"
our language has given the same to the parts
of our furniture. Also "back." And "seat."
These terms bridge worlds,
they begin in our houses and end (*if* they end)
in the hymn-worthy mansions of heaven
—and this association was here as soon as the word
was here: "chair" comes from the Latin "cathedra,"
and counts, as cousin, "cathedral." Though it's difficult
at times to remember this kinship with the numinous.
For example: chairs and even six-person benches
made completely from the joindered horns of cattle
and goats. Or the way the dominatrixes get paid
to use their slaves as human coffee tables and footstools.

———————

The first of the many McDonald's Happy Meal toys
that Jeremy received with his McNuggets
was a doodad from a merchandised cartoon called
Bobby's World, where the eponymous boy-hero sits
in the comfy hold of a purple pillowy armchair,
lost enchantedly in a children's book about
astronauts. But look: you can swivel him
out of sight on a plastic spindle, and up to take
his place is yet another Bobby, this one
in the futuristic-silver suit of a spaceman, with
a panel of rocket cockpit shown behind him. You
can turn the boy and the dream-boy into one another
all day, sweetly, seriously, until they blend
in the ecstasy of Ezekiel's flaming wheels.

———————

In the ecstatic visions of Gertrude of Helfta (middle/late
thirteenth century), she was admitted to the level of heaven
where Christ waits with his "honeyed mouth"; he
escorted her into the "bridal chamber." This was no
apparitional tryst, but conjugal in the fleshiest sense.
And Swedenborg's heaven, five centuries later, is neighborhoods
of houses: "like the dwellings on earth which we call homes,
they have rooms and bedrooms and courtyards," and
a wedding celebration there includes "tables with bread and crystal cups."
That was his idea: that it all went on, a version
of physicality went on beyond the grave, like the ditsy waves
of *I Love Lucy* through the universe after the television
is turned off—only solid, textured. This heaven of his . . .
you can knock for luck on actual wood.

———————

The drippy-nosed parishioners of a British church
in the thirteenth century likely knew less ease for their anatomy
than did Swedenborg's celestial beings. Even the barest
interior of a church included an altar (stone)
with canopy and frontal, a font (stone too),
a wooden bier, and a number of pennants, candles,
images of the Virgin and saints. "Conspicuously missing
were any benches, chairs, and pews; the congregation stood
[or] sat on the floor." Would any of them
have sprawled there on the cold straw
in a cold draft, looking hard-eyed and begrudgingly
at the silver vessel used to hold the bread of the Communion?
And it might be banded in ivory as well.
Furniture for the body of Christ.

———————

"Angels"—what I read in quickly skimming through a poem
of Linda Pastan's. I'll say now: there are continuums
connecting the most striking pairs of opposites.
Marriage is only the commonest example. Or the body
of a hermaphrodite. Centaurs. Flying fish.
Mermaids. Sleep. Of course Jesus. In-laws.
But in this case it was the voice of my Grandma Rosie,
dead now fortysome years, from when I was six or seven:
"Albie, finish your lox on bagel now. It's
time to go to *shul* and pray for Grandpa." Yes,
because *that's* what the word was—"bagels."
Those most shimmering elementals of all of Creation
were given an earthly link. Sometimes I think
I see them cavorting around the rim of that yeasty rink.

7. The Furniture Makers Have Three Patron Saints

Thank you for the shield-back chair and the ladder-back chair
    and the shepherdess chair. Thank you
for the look-chair with its padded rail, and thank you
    for the warming chair we scoot up to the fireplace
on bitter nights. For the bended-back chair
    we offer our thanks. The rocking and the easy.
For the folding, patio, lounge, and wingback,
    beanbag, arm-, side-, swivel-,
slat-back, comb-back, fan-back, banister-back,
    for hoop-back and for loop-back.
For recliner. For airliner. For those chairs
    in the earliest Mickey Mouse cartoons
that dance on festive, rubbery legs,
    we beam our thanks your way, for the chair
of the Pope and the chair of the slim-ankled bar girl.
    For the golden chair that clinked to the touch
of Midas's golden undershorts. And for the chair
    my grandmother died in painlessly,
with the slightly fearful but also expectant look
    of someone strapped in to a roller-coaster car.
And for the bones in us, that endo-chair
    born into a woman, into a man
—we thank you, Saint Victor, Saint Joseph, Saint Anne.

Especially we must thank you
    for the interface between the beatific
and the ordinary, even the mundane.
    "The first recorded drawers were used to file
church documents"—you see? The realm
    of "deity," of "soul," and of "transcendence," here
alloying with an object of practical use. How could we *not*
    be agog at that marriage?—how
its evidence is everywhere; how "the formalized dress
    of the servers, the incantatory nature of their speech,
and the nearly liturgical cast of the menu" makes
    a ritual of near-religious aspect for the congregated
under the sign of the Golden Arches, and haven't we all
    presented ourselves for respite
at the Counter and the Booth? And for the seater
    in the shape of a duck-billed hamburger
we thank you: let the kids play for a blessed while
    out of our hair. We thank you for so many variations:
table that's an emptied mega-spindle
    of underground telephone cable; cabinet of popsicle sticks
and beer cans. Someone's had a desk constructed
    to accommodate her new assistant kneeling in it,
out of sight, to attend to her intimate yearns; somebody
    else, a desk from which a gilded, gemmed ceramic statue
of the Virgin Mary pops up at a button's press
    as perky as a prairie dog. For these,
and all the "these" they represent, and for the nuptial bed
    Ulysses carved from the heart of an oak, its legs
still part of the tree and rooted down into that other
    heart in the liquid iron deeps of the planet.
We thank you for ottoman, settee, chaise lounge, divan,
    Saint Victor, Saint Joseph, Saint Anne.

There's that story of the evil duke/count/empress
     and the evil bed: a guest too short
was forcibly stretched to fit it, and a guest too long. . . .
     Deliver us from such horror.
Please protect us from the bed of rancor,
     save us from the bed of glacial sheeting.
There are desks of such unboundaried, monstrous power,
     with such sheen, that lives like ours
are just the rags by which those surfaces are polished
     . . . please. Deliver us from these.
And from the judge's bench, release us.
     From the table in the light of the surgical cutters and probers,
yes, and from the slow chair and its slow time
     in the waiting room . . . deliver us
back to our ongoing lives, and from us
     ask for any gift for you or those in your protection.
There are chairs in rooms where the questions are asked
     with rope and a rubber hose . . . please
don't forsake us. From the spy eyes
     in the government's sleepless hallways of computer hutches . . .
please, deliver us. Please deliver us
     safe, on time, according to plan.
Movers of the human spirit,
     deliver us in your shimmering van.
Haul us, then install us in place,
     Saint Victor, Saint Joseph, Saint Anne.

8.

In just a few minutes the cleanup crew,
and dozens of neighborhood residents, and idle gawkers,
and shift two from the TV news, will break this
dreamy moment she's been given, of wandering solitary
around the devastation, of . . .
"communing" is the closest I can come to what
she's doing: every jagged fragment
seems to hold the screams,
the psalms, the devotional lilt,
of over seven thousand years
encoded in it, like the genome
woven into every cell. Here, look . . .
the pitiful crumbs of the main hall's tile mosaic,
so tiny and granular: almost the aerosol of a tile mosaic.
And here . . . the thick and heavy wooden platform
where the Torah gets unscrolled is now
a drift of wooden sand. *Well, what do I know?*
Maybe the dream of a heavy wooden platform is to be exploded
into particles so small that they can ride the wind
like spirits. (Yes, and maybe the dream of a spirit
is thick and nasty: it wants to be a bed.) And
here . . . she bends with fevered concentration. Here
are slivers of that very same Elijah's chair they used
at Jeremy's circumcision ritual almost twenty years ago.
(The chair proportioned to an infant, that he'd sit on
while the cantor intoned and the *mohel* readied the instruments,
and then he'd be lifted out of it, and—as the specialized blade
began its work—the prophet Elijah would sit in it next,
benignly overseeing.) As the chair was sized
to Jeremy when he was eight days old and living,
now that Jeremy's dead, is who-knows-where, these
small remainders of what might be called the corpse of a chair
seem sized to Jeremy still. She slips one,
toothpick-light, in her sweatshirt pocket. "Excuse
me, Ms. . . ."—those others start to invade the scene,
and she leaves. That's all. I wish there were something
more melodramatic to end with: that she
drops to her knees like a tree on fire and raves
until the flames have eaten her clean. *That*

would be a good one. Or a weeping
that's kept secret inside the cabinet of her sternum.
Even that. But no, she goes home,
and the years pass, as the years do
whether we're vigilant or not. And every Passover,
at the *seder* with Scott and Michelline and Trishie,
at the part near the end where the door
is ceremoniously opened and the prophet Elijah
welcomed into the house, she slips
that sliver from its silver-inlaid memorial box and sets it,

a chair, at their table.

Mine

Won't Let Go

This afternoon I'm obliged to attend a birthday party
for Rachel (three) at McDonald's, where the playroom
chutes and slides, in their cartoony blue and red,
are like the circulatory system of an anatomy text,
but huged up to the size of conveyor tubes
at a major granary. Next week, it's my nephew Ian's
bar mitzvah. On the 27th, Lois's daughter's wedding.
These rituals won't let go. Can't you feel a funeral
is throwing open its closet door and thinking, "Hmm,
I haven't tried on *this* severe black dress in a while, this one
with the wide and ragged fingernail scrapes across the breast
for a display of grief"? And it X's a date on the calendar.

———————

At the worst, he'd scrub his hands, then slit the skin
of his arm *just so* to keep a count, then scrub the blood
off his hands, then cut at his arm again, then scrub
. . . extreme, for even OCD. But every repetition
kept the world (*his* world, in any case) in order,
no less so than when the mile line of priests
in masks of sheeted gold and lapis sings its slow way
to the temple, and the *one-to-send* is bound upon
the *send-stone*, with his chest undone and spread
like wings, and his live heart torn from the root
—so that the seasons will continue to wheel, the beasts
will bear in their proper time, and Earth fit into the cosmos.

———————

Finally, after the little oozy coils of soft-serv sundaes
and the candles, Ronald McDonald Himself appeared
in gifts-dispensing, Popish, rajahn, bozo majesty.
Later they told me what he said to the birthday girl
was "I make playing fun," but at the time I *did* see
ingots of silver cloud and a suffusion of light
escape like free electrons from his body: "I
make rain and sun" as mixed through party squawktalk.
Look, I know: he pimps for hamburgers; that's not the job
of a god. And yet the children were three, then thirteen,
and the snow turned to grass, and the grass became air,
and somewhere there was a tree with one black leaf for everybody.

Sung Grievously

My back gives out and the thrown bolt tears through nerve
from brain to cock in the pop of a fingersnap that lasts
a year per nanosecond. And that was just tying
my shoe. Maneuvering gingerly into the seat of my Toyota
is a fathoms-deep and dangerous self-assignment, of the kind
we usually associate with diving bells and oxygen helmets.
It turns out that the body is a macromicrointerconnective
oneness (what we always "know" and yet equally never
"remember"), every molecule of peptide, say, or dopamine
initiating ever-outward vectors of inevitable force
along the ball-&-socket, jack-&-outlet, straw-&-spark
causationweb, throughout the threaded mollusc shells,
and the marrow-and-fat-stuffed ziti, of the body;
and soon it registers as a sear-mark in the heart or genitalia

—the way the textbooks say a ladybug migration rises
skyward like a hundred thousand marks of punctuation
in the Andes, and this spritzle of disturbance sets off necessary series
of events that finally climax as a crop-destroying hail
in Nebraska, shaking stone dice in your skull all night.
A friend who works the cop beat for the local paper says
"There's no such creature as 'asymptomatic murder'"
—even the least of the toe-tagged John Does in the freezer
is a story, is a roadkill on the good reporter's Infoway
of Narrative, "and some," she adds ". . . well, let me put it
this way: there are bums in Pauper's Field, and there are headlines
every day from Capitol Hill, and sometimes . . . you know . . .
certain theories account for both of those; there are connections."
With a noir, mysterioso, "snoopy knowledge" look, she leaves me

thinking about the Garden of Eden. It wasn't a *trés* lush chunk
of rock free-floating the universe. It was part of a system
that *we* call a planet; and when those two Originals
betrayed their native innocence, and were banished
into the woes of the greater world . . . that world was waiting
for them. It wasn't deifically abracadabra'd
out of dung and bile at the moment of the apple-bite,
no; it had been there, sharing the moon and clay and oxygen
with Eden all along. The unyielding ground to plow
in stingy rows: was waiting. And the grinding-stone:
was waiting. She would heavily carry the fruit of their lust
in unease, and give birth in pain. And he
would enter the field now, and bend to the labor that stings
the eyes and makes the back sing grievously.

Reentry

(Also, I Know a Man Who Keeps His 1934 Remington Typewriter Oiled and Clean as If the World Depended upon Its Utility)

By the beehived dolls and slickum'd ducks-assed dudes
who hope to engineer some slither in their otherwise spazmoidal
attempts at The Swim, The Jerk, The Pony, The Roach, The Peppermint Twist,
a student of danceology can tell you "1961-to-65," and anybody
this side of legally blind can tell you truly these are huffing
fortysomethings who have rented their former high school gym
for yet one more inane sock-hop reunion. It's a fact:
you *can't* go home again (same river twice, etc.); and if home is a body,
some of us restructuring The Stroll,
The Locomotion, The Watusi, never lived there
at ease to begin with. Not that this cold pour
of realism's waters is enough to douse the glimmering allure
of What Once Was: and by the great prohibitive bandolier-like X
of flaming swords God sets across the Gates, we know

return is one of the original urges, passed down
undiluted from that mythic proto-twosome, to our own enduring
neuroarchitected need for viable reentry
into the hundreds of tiny elusive edens
we desire daily. "It's like . . . sometimes I go all wild, and want,"
says gay pal Leigh about her ladylove, "to crawl deep into her
on all fours, slip some funky umbilical hookah-tube inside my lips,
and curl up there in the mamaswamp"—a want
that's *everybody's* story, albeit in Leigh's own sexualspeak.
Who *hasn't* sensed the neocortex yearn to disevolve and flow
back down the pipes, into the brain stem? Michelangelo's
"first accomplished piece of sculpture" he made marketable
as ancient Greek by rubbing dirt into its hairline cracks:
what Petrarch calls "the radiance of the past." Just twenty-five lines

ago, between the lines, I opted out of another round of The Fly
and The Mashed Potatoes. On the front steps, under an overflowing
punchbowl of a moon, a woman I haven't seen in thirty-one years
says, ". . . anyway, we were divorced last June. The thing is,
I still visit him on weakwilled nights—we fight, we screw, O Jesus.
It's bad, I know, it's . . . 'counterproductive.' But
the pain we made together, when the marriage was at its bottommost
. . . I've never been *that* alive since." Then after a beat of silence:
"How do I climb out of this?" *I* couldn't guess. And even so,
I recognize the saving trick of those who have learned to internalize
that X of flaming swords. It's like this: somewhere deep inside,
you touch its fireblazing shape, and somewhere deep inside
it sears you with the word *no*. And you turn and go
out into the difficult dance of the world: The Now, The Here, The Passing.

Rembrandt / Panties

A couple is having a vitriolic lulu
of an argument at the corner of Fitch and Applegate,
a hackles-raiser, chainsaws-of-adrenalin,
all-out squallabaloo. I can't hear a word, too bad
—my Nissan's windows: shut, the AC: on—but
one-tenth of their bodyspeech would be enough
to signify "ferocity" with clarity
to any sentient bioform, terrestrial or extra-.
First, *she* indicates she's going to flick
his puttywad of a brain from his skull, and launder it,
with venomous shoots of energy, on a quaint old-fashioned washing board
she'll wear across her belly like a jug-band musician. Next,
he indicates the vast encumbrance of her sourpussish spite
(it's about the length of the travel of lightwaves
through the universe) and how he intends to break this
over his knee in one clean snap as if its tonnage were only
a nougat bar. This dialogue continues
as the red turns green, and I drive on to Shop-n-Save
and shop (the *save* is arguable), and by the time
I speed back to that corner, they're leaning against each other,
faces slobbered in each other's necks, and heaving
with the deep breaths of some governing emotion
I can't guess at from my windowed distance.
Anger still, become a standoff wrestling match?
A segue into something vaguely tender? Lust?
Vampiric feeding? Simple resignation to a stagnancy
beyond all change? I don't know
and I'll never know, the way it is
with Rembrandt's self-(and most unguarded)portrait
from the last year of his life, the one in which he glances up at us
in midwork at his easel, and the face we see is something
like a splat of tallow, laughing—that's right,
laughing, from that sunken-in
puff-pastry of a face. By now he's broke

(the auctioneers have emptied out his house,
to the least cheese plate and parrot cage) and broken,
in all of the hammering ways a set of days can repeatedly
beat at the spirit . . . and he's *laughing,*
carefree, uncontained. Unless
he laughs more bitterly than this, or more insanely,
or he's acting out the part of someone else, or
. . . we don't know, and we can't reconcile
what we think we see here, with the sour, shabby
facts of his old age. A page in a catalogue
I received today describes a book "in nearly mint condition,
only one word underlined in the text": it doesn't say
which word, and when I called . . . the book was sold already.
I'm thinking about the night I stopped my car
along the dark, grassed sand dunes east of here
and found a pair of black bikini panties
at the roadside, it was dropped from the height of a secret plot
I wasn't allowed to follow. It might have been a story
of ecstasy. It might have been the kind of grief
that burns out of existence an entire node of the memory.
I only knew that it was here, a testament
to the power of X, and delicate under the slow turn
of the equally unreadable stars.

A Photo of a Lover from My Junior Year in College

Or the Earth: one half in sun,
one half in darkness.

The planet can be its two selves at once.
Not us; we're either asleep, or awake.

We're either walking over the countless graves,
or in them. Here, or there.

We rarely pay attention to the moment of transition.
Blood, being oxygenated. Love, when it's still just chemicals.

She has one of her arms in an arm of her blouse,
and the other one wonderfully not.

Goliath and the Barbarians

Even the atom is a tension
between its heart and its orbits.
It begs to be split.
Just look at the diagrams.

The ocean begs to be air, the air
to be ocean. When I "made love" once
in the roll of the surf . . . we *were* the surf:
a mix of both; then parting.

——————

As if "man" and "woman" weren't enough.
"Me" and "them." "Innocent" and "guilty."
As if ethical plasticity along a sliding scale
weren't conflicting enough, there needs to be these

sharp, bathetic cries of solicited loyalty
from the poems of an anthology: the work
of *haute*-clown Kenneth Koch, with every word
the hurdy-gurdied BANG-poof of a circus gun;

the tight work of Louise Glück, every word
a further paper cut that shrinks beneath the sting
of antiseptic. As if "sub-" and "supra-" weren't enough
like rival posters spieling the fight

between the brain's dank, remnant, lizard center
and the airy, sunlit Great Plains
of its neocortex. "Sanctioned" and "taboo." And also
"fidelity" and "betrayal"—not to mention

the gray farina in between, that place
where moral zip codes shade from one state into the next,
that uncommitted patch of inner slush
my friends and I, my colleagues, family, national leaders

and I, have homesteaded ever since the (*slap!*)
birth-cry that couldn't decide
if it were celebration or pain. Who *doesn't* stand around
like Steve Reeves in *Goliath and the Barbarians,*

tied with each arm to a horse that pulls him
opposite directions? Or the less pretentious image
of a breakfast roll that's torn. And something
—call it steam; but *something*—rises spectrally into the day

the way it did at the first mitosis.

Invisible

The parents are fucking. The parents are discussing
whether or not the soul is ever in complicitous alliance
with the external world. The parents are arguing
garden green or *sand* for the bathroom
wallpaper (maybe you wouldn't be surprised how much
ferocity attaches to those differences).
The two-year-old is oblivious. The parents build
a hill of salt on which they writhe and slice themselves,
the two-year-old is crawling blithely through it
as if it doesn't exist. The crimson pillars
of sexual moan they raise throughout the house
are only empty air to him. (We all live in cities
to which we're unconscious, stride across
the warrens of the dead with less awareness
than the roaches in our shadows have.) In two years
they've been sensitized to wake at any rustle
from their child's crib, but slumber through
the plaintive lengths of sound the freight train
excavates through the thickly packed night.

———————

The giddy paleontologists are deservedly thrilled with this
impressive bone the size of a cannon;
and, right there at the site, with dust
the color of cow dung still in their teeth, ears, hair,
they break out their bottle of cheap champagne
and seven plastic glasses, and they toast themselves
and their Cretaceous souvenir, elated despite
the sun that kilns their skin and a wind that mourns
through the rocks like the call of a train,
a long phantasmal banner. Sun
and emptiness and a *T. rex* bone: that's what they see,
it's all we can expect these seven diligent men to see,
although they stand on sacred tribal ground,
in a city of gods, with timeless godly presence
all about them. They've defiled this land. The find
is theirs or isn't theirs: the law will decide,
which is also a vast, invisible architecture.

And finally the fossil is "jacketed" for removal
in burlap and plaster; in a single and finicky, levered haul
it's lifted 70 million years into the future.
I suppose that's loosely—very loosely—like
the transposition that a pharaoh and his populace believed in:
rising out of death itself, into the fields
of forever. Of course they expected even forever to be
familiar. Tombware isn't just symbolic
golden gaudery, but also simple bowls, stone knives,
and toilets(!) for the afterlife: as if
our body's systems necessarily imply a certain logical response,
and nothing else can be imagined. Yes—except
so many pharaohs *have* been untombed into a future
wholly alien to them. They watch the gawking
of museum-goers—less a kindred life-form than the offering-cattle
that once paraded past them. Also, mummies were used
to stoke the engines of nineteenth-century railroad trains.
We'll all be smoke, we'll all be pressed to oil,
all be recombined in a place, in a series of places, we can't guess
the laws of physics or periodic table of elements for.
We'll all be Mars, we'll all be rain.
Rain: the story we'd know, if only we understood
—in *our* world's terms—
the code of those tapping knuckles.

Aerothermal photos, snapping subtle heat differential
from an airplane's height, have mapped dark smudges
of cities so lost, so underground/ . . . but
this is only an indirect way of saying a lover
recognizes absence in the slight signs left behind:
a relic intimacy the sheets still hold, a trilobite
of lipstick on a glass's rim. And what *was* in her brain
for their three iffy years of marriage?—what
alternative domains contained the shining, sky-high
spiderwebbish walkways of the twenty-second century, or possibly
the brutal dark of caves, with such insistence
that they finally seemed more real, overbalancingly
real, than this small suburban house? Somehow
he'll have to tell the two-year-old: the parents
are divorcing. You can stroke a head to sleep and still
not understand the universe an inch behind its eyes.
We *think* we "see" the stylized train of captured cattle,
lapis stones, acacia, pond ducks heaped in hummocks, eunuched slaves
paraded past a pharaoh's steady gaze in tomb art, but
our eyes are about as distant from his as they are
from a queen bee's polygons. Out the window a girl,
looks seventeen, is skateboarding, evidently
through a place her headphones structure: now she shimmies,
dips, leaps, lip-synchs, spirals, zigzags
past the pinnacles and deeps of a hermetic world.

———————

A train's been traveling through this poem,
and a bird is threading its way through the train,
and a berry is journeying through the bird,
is carrying the DNA of berries in infinitude,
back to the soil. It rains. The smear of guano
liquefies and enters the earth,
the home-of-homes, the alpha and omega,
the transubstantiater of bones. One day
I visit Waldheim Cemetery: my parents are here,
a little above the dinosaurs, a little below
the last spilled tangerine light of this August dusk.
They're here, with Uncle Lou, and Grandma Rosie, and everyone else
they were with on the surface, together again. It's a regular
retirement community down there, and I wish we'd buried them
the way the dead of Egypt were, with meaningful *objets*,
so that a klatch of bones could meet on every Thursday night,
and play with a deck of bone poker cards for a pot
of bone nickels, and laugh again at the same stale jokes.
That's all just fancifulness, I know: a way of saying things
that seems "poetic." But the dead *are* down there,
freed from time. And we can't see,
but they can of course,
the stilts
on which we walk through their cities.

Canyon, Gorge, Arroyo

*The seventeenth-century bibliophile George Thomason, whose specialty
was seditious tracts, once buried his collection of over 22,000 publications,
fearing their discovery by the army. What if he'd died before he was able to
retrieve them?*

How many other codices
and folios are stored down there,
are held in geologic strata? — pages
that, in trading earth for air, no longer turn.
They're like the minute-lines that mark a clock:
time moves, but they stay unmoved.

———————

My Grandpa Louie isn't only *in* the earth,
by now he *is* the earth, is atomically one with it,
and so is all of the Old World sensibility that made him
so mysterious to me: the way he took tea
through a cube of sugar gripped in his yellowing front teeth,
and the Russian tavern songs he'd hum along
to the hand-cranked music box.
The Yiddish-language newspaper that he read, however,
is still being published — barely.
I imagine its latest sad gray passenger-pigeon-of-an-issue
pacing circles on his grave, impatient, waiting to fold
its paper wings and join him in the darkness,
maybe cover his chest,
as when — in life — he'd fall asleep under its pages.

———————

Canyon, gorge, arroyo—we can see
at any cleft in the earth, it's text
on text the whole way down.
It's shelving.
And someone else may tell us that this
is an archeologist tenderly brushing the dust
from a buried line of inscription, or a paleontologist
tending to a row of fossil pocks, but we
can recognize a librarian when we see one.

―――――――

We think of death as Nothing, as a stillness and a void,
but it's an active, endless hunger:
of the countless thousands
of third-millennium Hittite hieroglyphic documents,
"none has survived for our finding," done as they were
in ink on linen-backed tablets of wood.
In Time's salivas, a thing like that
dissolves like a peppermint lozenge. Occasionally,
a relic does float into the present moment:
we have ancient Incan quipus—stout main cords
and slenderer ancillary threads, on which a code
of knots served adequately as a kind of writing (cousin
to the rosary and the fringe of the Jewish *tallis*).
One, recovered from a chieftan's tomb, is *ten pounds*
of transmitted fact. Ten pounds of knots,
as if to remind us what it means for a nervous system
to carry our complicated lives.

―――――――

And did you dream?
I dreamt. I dreamt I visited
Grandpa Louie's grave.
　　You visited Grandpa Louie's grave.
　　Did you enter it?
I entered it, I was there in the must,
I wandered the city
architected of bone and the ghosts of electrical pulses.
　　And what did you see?
His life. His Jewghetto immigrant life
that had always seemed more distant to me
than the toppled columns of ancient Rome
and the Babylonian ziggurats.
　　And did you understand what you saw?
I understood what I saw. At last, I felt at home
in the gutturals of his Yiddish speech,
among the cracked leather straps of his phylacteries,
and the watch fob, and the feathered splay
of chicken-pluck in the wooden bowl.
　　You say at last you understood?
I spread apart the shut halves of his ribcage
and I studied.
I could read him like an open book.

A Cup

Toward the end, when the pain from the cancer
was a slag heap, was an active, growing termite hill of pain,
my mother asked God to take her out of this world.
For weeks He didn't respond. "Why—aren't I good enough?":
a sentence now like a wire in my heart that won't cool off.
But she kept asking, kept inviting Him into her room
among its stained sheets and its maze of useless tubes.
Her voice was only a dying teakettle on the empty
Siberian steppes. But she was insistent, and genuine.
Even so, it wasn't like the Vegas-wattage invitations

other places sent out. In the temple of Apollo at Argos,
one a month, a virgin, "she-the-chosen," lapped the fresh blood
from a slaughtered lamb, and then the god was in her,
and she prophesied. *And still, my mother continued
her frail request for His alleviating presence.* In the eighth
—the highest—tower of the sanctuary of Bel,
there was a spacious temple, and in it was a great bed,
draped in gold, and here the consort of that Babylonian deity
waited, naked: and then sex was like one two-pronged strike
of lightning through their bodies. *Nonetheless, my mother*

*wouldn't halt the whistle in her thick, corroded lungs,
her imploration. Her signal—I'm ready.* In a way, the whole
of what we are is either a sign for stop
or welcome. Mauling at his own face with a talismanic
Kodiak paw, and with it scoring lines like wet red staves
across his nipples . . . thus, the shaman—"the beseecher"—
re-creates himself to be *so* fiercely radiant in ritual abasement
that the gods can finally see, and they home in along the beam
he emits, they weight his head with a knowledge of heaven,
and this he brings to his people. *Yes, and even when compared*

to that *dramatic gouging-out of body entranceways,*
my mother persisted in tiny, and sometimes silent, whimpers
saying her preparedness. Some days I'd swear the history
of the planet was nothing but one enormous chorus of voices
singing a clamorous opera by Beckon and Woo. There's a petal
evolved to resemble a cross between a mink stole
and a landing strip, and this entices bees the way the slither
of the stripper's slowly, *slowly* skin-descending zipper
hypnotizes (hip-&-rump-&-thighnotizes) eyes that form
a single syncopated swarm of voyeuristic pleasure

in the darkened theater air. The salt lick calls the deer,
the sugar-water feeder lures the hummingbird. An elder
sits all night at the grave with a platter of grain and embers
—his antenna, his reception dish—and just before the dawn,
a throng of the ancestors whisper their wisdoms. Though the airwaves
must be very jammed, eventually my mother received
her answer. *What was left of her rose out of her,*
a little whuff of steam. And then the nurses tidied up,
as if it were all a matter of crumbs and rumpled napkins.
She'd been heard, I guess. It wasn't like a rajah

in his howdah at the head of a parade of temple elephants
shouting *look! look!* to the skies; still, it sufficed.
I've read a report on various pilgrims to Jerusalem: and
there, where the holy fires are lit, and the word
is the Word, and the grand mosques and the synagogues
send heavenward their pleadings for redemption on a huge cloud
of a thousand accumulated breaths, "an English woman
in the 1930's went daily to the Mountain to welcome
the Lord's return with a nice cup of tea." But
she meant it; she was steeped in it.

Suitcase Song

John-O was given a key to the apartment. The deal
was this: if Phil died suddenly, and John-O heard,
he would rush on over, enter the apartment, leave
unseen with Phil's brown suitcase, and secretly pitch it
into the mounded deeps of the city dump.
Simply, there were things that Phil didn't want
to hurt his family with. Do you have *yours?*
I have *mine.* The brown suitcase. Sasha's sister,
on her deathbed—dinky, frail, just a mild
skim-milk trickle of a hospice patient—
tensed, sat up, and unloosed
such confessional invective that it seemed the walls
and the sheets would have to be splattered in shit,
her cancer having acted with the harsh, disbursing
force of a tornado on the brown and hard-shelled
suitcase in her electrochemical memory webs.
Is yours secure? from love? from sodium pentathol?
Last year, when a tornado hit our fringe
of downtown businesses, the air was alive for counties around
with the downward dance of naked canceled checks,
handwritten notes, hotel receipts, e-mail transcripts,
smeary Polaroids, a swirl of lacy underwisps
that jellyfished the skies, and from The G-Spot Shoppe
a rain of plastic pleasure aids, of which one prime example
pierced a cow between the eyes and struck her dead.

————————————

Maybe AIDS—I wasn't sure. But he was dying,
that was sure: as dry as a stick of human chalk,
and making the terrible scritch-sound of a stick of chalk,
in his throat, in the community air, in the room
across from Sasha's sister. Something . . . *hidden*
in the trace of rundown aura still around him
as we chatted there one morning . . . a tv? a sissyboy tv?
I wasn't sure, but it was obvious
his life-chalk held a story not yet written,
not confessed yet
for this storyniverous planet.
And when I remembered my mother's own
last days . . . the way a person is a narrative,
the strength of which is either
revelation or withholding. It was summer, and the garden
at the nursing home was fat with summer's pleasures:
flowered mounds like reefs of coral,
bees as globular as whole yolks.
In her room, my mother disappeared a breath
at a time, and everything else was only a kind of scenery for that.
The wink of pollen in the light. The birds. Their feather-lice.
The bursting spores. Those opened-up
cicada husks abandoned on the patio
—the small, brown, unlocked luggage
that's completed its work in this world.

Rarefied

This sweater is made from only the finest, softest underhairs of the Mongolian camel.
—From a mail-order catalogue

"Fancy-schmancy," my father would have said,
whose snazziest sweater was still a déclassé
synthetic from the sweatshops of Taiwan. My friend
Deloris, however, who really owns such clothes,
would say "exquisite" or "sublime"—her opened closet's
row of shoulders teases late-day bedroomlight
along *such* textures, there are days when the laboring brain
and throbbing crotch appear to us to be not much more
than her wardrobe's tasteful accessories. ". . . woven
from genital-down of prepubescent yeti, and then
hand-sewn in our undersea domes." "Untouched
by anyone other than albino elves, this wool is. . . ."

Rarefied—to Helthi Hart, the diet guru, it's
a cup of clear organic cauliflower broth. And for
the Emperor Excessia, it's a mad dessert of swans' tongues
—there were, what? ten thousand?—dipped in a slip
of stiffening honey and set out to await the banqueteers
like a field of fresh shoots they could graze.
Some Roman party hosts had great roped bowls of snow
brought from the mountaintops to entertain their guests
with dishes of rose-petal sherbet and chilled roe.
They might even allow the household slaves to slide
leftover snow along the burning welts the ropes ate
into their shoulders all down the mountainside.

Afterward it was an unrecognizable tatter.
But an image of my father's worn-thin Bargain City
"all-weather" jacket is still whole in its polyester glory.
This is what happened: the alley dog (he later called the thing
a "cur") had cornered Livia, and she screamed once,
with a seven-year-old's unselfconscious terror.
And then my father was there, with his jacket wound around his arm,
and a rock. When it was over, he tore the sleeves off, tied the poor dog
quiet and, after comforting Livia, they both kneeled down
to comfort the dog. He was like that. And the jacket
that served as weapon and restraint?—was like him,
every day of his life. It did what was needed.

———————————

I misread "migraine." Which of the two
would we call the most rarefied? "Margarine"?
Or maybe comparison isn't the point. A ghost
is a person rarefied through the fine, fine colander
death; that doesn't make, for most of us, extinction
an ideal. It was hard to think of Frank and Deloris
divorcing, since it was hard to imagine the two of them
engaging in *anything* so mundane as sex or rage or envy
with the rest of the hoi polloi. They seemed unearthly
in close to a literal way, like radio waves. And yet divorce
they did. They found *something* real they could unjoin,
hertz from hertz until there just was air.

———————————

A dream: We own the softest of the soft
Mongolian camel underhair sweaters. One day
(we *think* we're doing the "right thing") we release it
into the wild, to romp with its brother and sister
desert sweaters, out where it "belongs."
You know, however, what happens by now: it's unfit
to fend for itself amid that hardened herd.
They beat it. It's hungry. It crawls back
into the city, mewing, curling up at night against a door
my father opens and, seeing something in need, he brings it inside,
wraps it in flannel. That's how he was.
He'd give you the cheap shirt off his back.

Zenith

was the brand name, and that radio made
the man who'd be my father in another twenty years
one very mesmerized and nearly acolyte-attentive
ten-year-old. *The Red Avenger.*
Ranger Ed and Dippy. Uncle Leonard's Rayolene Singalong Hour.
Otherwise, it would have been the usual
stupid, summer-blistered streetside entertainment
that Chicago flung like stale crumbs
to an immigrant Yidboy—mumblety-peg,
cadging a ride on the ice cart. Yes, but
this, *this* . . . at the first, they didn't *have* words
for the depth of their astonishment. *Talking!*
Talking, from the air! The night they brought it home
and plugged it in, and the dial lit,
and the woe of invisible
Russian violins filled up the living room, the woman
who'd be my grandmother in another twenty years
fell to her knees and rocked, she beat at her ears
with her fists in a kind of wonder,
as if this were the bush
on fire, and lo!, it was not consumed,
the Voice spoke, yet it was not consumed.

It's still in the family. Sixty years, and endless
techno-newness later, endless spates of changed tastes,
but it's here, like the mummy
untombed in some movie, speaking
scratchily still, from out of its dusts,
beyond its proper time.
This once deluxe and cutting-edge
"cathedral-style" 1930s Zenith Hitone
channels, now, our most postmodern hipglitz cyber-rock
through such encrypting auditory fuzz
it may as well be *Colonel Jones's Showtime Talent Search.*
Nurse Sarah's Secret Diary. The Creeper.
Maybe . . . listen . . . it *is.* Maybe short-term
memory is shot, and all that remains is the long,
long waves of the past being reeled in.
The Quiz Boys. Theater Time. Sheriff of Prairie Gulch . . .
they're a spirit community now,
a gabble of ghosts in the vacuum tubes.

———————

I lied. I thought it "sounded good"
for a poem. She *didn't* fall to her knees
in a mystified awe. In fact,
by then she'd already seen
what the point of a saber can do to a sister's belly,
how the loose intestine
lifted over the head of one of the tsar's "Jewraper" soldiers
for a trophy can undo the whole of a universe;
she'd already traveled out of that land
to this one, in the stinkhole of a ship,
in the odor of ship rats
and a hundred unwashed human bodies,
waxy and bacterially rank. She'd
been around, and toughened. Love
and duty of various kinds had sucked her nipples
swollen, and had calloused the soft of her hands.
She'd seen such things . . . !—a stone
would weep from them, a stone would sing
as piteously as the angels. And so this wood box
with its noises . . . it meant nothing to her,
just another American *tchotchke*. Right;
as if *I* know. As if my single photon
of imagination can burrow through death
to reveal her life. So maybe she *was* astounded
as a wave of Brahms or her first insurance commercial
issued out of that unexplainable contraption.
And those two conflicting grandmothers
overlap, the way that two shows sometimes will
on a mistuned radio
—a palimpsest of megahertz.

———————————

And *would* my father have known the literal definition
of "zenith," then or ever—its specific
astronomical association? No. Not that
emburdened and unbookish man. For him, it was enough
to beat his head against the wall of the world
each week, and offer a smear of his blood
for the signing of his paycheck. If he read
at all, it was only the instruction
Support Your Family written ceaselessly with a nib
dipped in his marrow, in his spit,
in the chemical flashes that the retinas play games with
through the night, even when the eyelids are closed.
And so a word like "zenith" only led a life of metaphor
for him—if that; for him, and his and my mother's
neighborhood friends. They couldn't have told you
that a "paragon" is a grade of diamond,
"benchmark" is a term in tidal surveys, or
a "pinnacle" comes from Gothic architecture
—although half of them, at the least, would have at some time
owned a radio with one of those names.
The more we're here, the more we lose
our contact with the primacy. And then
what's left?—a "general sense of things,"
a secondary level, something like this poem:
nostalgia. Once, I asked Dan Nussbaum
if he knew what "pinnacle" was, and he
corrected my pronunciation.
"You don't know? It's a card game."

_____

Writing poems
is so immense a pleasure that it's shameful
to compare my "work" to his
depleting, grunt-around-the-city, door-to-door
insurance salesman job. I'm sure
he had entire days that would have served the OED
as a sidebar illustration for "duress." And yet
my hubris is: I often think of him, at the end
of one of my own unhappy-down-to-the-bone
collections of daylight hours. It's night
by then, I'm weary, and I see him
—though he should be even wearier—in a festively
energetic snit at the radio. "Albie, look: it's on
the fritz again. I fiddle with the knobs,
and still—kaput! I think I'm going
to have to operate on its *kishkes*." He's so
gleeful at this—another task! Another
being needed! And he starts
experimentally to tap at the glowing volume control.
Not that the radio's here. It serves
for what I want to say; I made it up.
As for my father . . . all I have is
an analogy of my father, a vision,
a vapory fossil lingering in the room
anachronistically—a chord
that's here, persistent,
although the station that beamed it is long off the air.

"The Great Ones

always make it look so easy."
— Sitcom second banana, as a sex god whips out his lighter and
   a sex goddess offers her cigarette

Thunderclaps (inside of which an intercontinental flight's a toothpick
in a Tarzan yell) and blasts of marrow-shivering electrical gashes
muscle in from the north: a weather appropriate to The Great Ones.
Maybe they'll favor us by uttering some echoing pronouncement
— ethics, stocks and bonds, world war, a really great new mousse
that's suddenly appeared for them as readily as manna fallen overnight.
While *we* climb over the side of the bed each morning, little cliff edge,
little lemming. While *we* cough gobs of lung-mess
into tissues and study these viscous shapes like soothsayers.
(*Bloodworms. Hummingbird bowels.* A drear prognostication.)
When The Great Ones labor, the dross of the world is alchemically
begreatened to match: Sir William Herschel, needy of a telescope mirror
three feet in diameter (with no existing foundry that would risk the task),
constructed himself an inexpensive mold of pounded horse dung,
as if his were a vision exalted enough to lift up such *rejecta*
into kinship with the stars. While the rest of us stumble about
and wonder how our own few burlap sacks of pared-off calluses
and menses-slough and hair-loss start to add up
toward a life. The Great Ones: "courage" comes to mind, then even that
intended adulation fails when I think of Mrs. Pankhurst
on a plank bed being funnel-fed
against her fervent hunger-striking wishes — four detectives
bear their bull strength on the struggling suffragette
to still her spasms, as a day-nurse works
a tube in and another pours
their pigmash down her forced throat (legal, alimentary
rape is what it comes to: and her own continued,
conscienceful refusal). While the rest of us
aren't always strong enough to lift the phone

for its single beetle of news, its single carrion beetle
bearing an ash of news in its chitinous horns
between the dark and the wires. And for how many words of his *Dictionary*
did Samuel Johnson personally write definitions
("plagued the while by ill health and the death of his wife,"
as one source puts it)?—43,500; while the two words
"cervical" "tumor" press their pincers into the gray myrrh of my brain,
and stay, and grow, and won't make room for any others. How many
runaways did Sojourner Truth deliver?—while today
the weight of the thought of my sister
strapped down in the hospital is an anvil in my head,
just her, you see how weak and small I am,
just that one pea-sized leak in the hull to worry about,
and I can't move—an anvil's in my head.
The Great Ones: oysters Rockefeller and plutonium,
The Great Ones: Mount Parnassus, and my tongue is so dry.
The Great Ones: silver chalices, so dry
I can't, The Great Ones: papal dispensation, dry I can't begin,
The Great Ones: shantung silk, I can't begin a prayer,
my tongue so dry I can't begin a prayer, The Great Ones:
sex in weightlessness above the Earth and civet musk and Pentateuch,
I can't begin a prayer to ask for anything,
The Great Ones: born absolved, The Great Ones: 60,000 television channels,
ask for anything, Olympic gold, Miss Universe, The Great Ones
carved of marble, ask for anything though if,
The Great Ones truffles and paté, I could,
though if I could, The Great Ones oratorio, The Great Ones
unanimity, though if I could I'd ask for something,
strong enough to lift the phone, The Great Ones: ships
with sandalwood and dancing apes, to add up toward a life,
The Great Ones: never grieve, or if they do
the heavens weep, to ask for something, manna, stars,
so modest as reprieve.

Ecstasy,

but not what you're thinking. Ecstasy originally: *ex*, "out of," +
histasthai, "to be standing": when some thunderbolt emotion
shatters you out of yourself. In ancient Greek calamities
—when Procne kills and dismembers her son, simmers
this chopmeat, serves it to her husband (the father)—
there's a snap of recognition so beyond the mind's
accommodation that a new, a second, mind is fissioned
out of the first: a coolly monster mind, to meet
the monstrous situation. And a researcher owns an archive
of thousands of photographs snapped at the pinpoint of disaster
—say, the red-scrolled roller-coaster car
uncoupling—and a second, see-through but recognizable person
sits beside the person. It looks like a trick of the light
at first: if the light had a mouth, and was screaming.

After eighteen hours of labor, Rebecca delivered twins
to the world on a rolled-out rug of silty uterine blood:
"At the final spasm, my consciousness floated above my body,"
meaning there was yet *another* umbilicus, spectral
ladder-rope of the psyche's, in that overcrowded room;
"look—aren't they *lovely?*" / A hooker, Rhonda tells me, does
the same: becomes a cloud above the automatic writhing. It's
what some of us do with entire swatches of childhood. /
Isn't *everyone* a duo? *Bound:* to leap away from; *bound:*
contained in place. / The Christian regent
Offa had his gold coins copied from earlier Arab models.
This explains why curly "abstract scribble" in a circle
around the central *Offa Rex* says that *Muhammad
is the prophet of God*. One gold coin. Two cosmologies.

"I *know* what you all call him: 'Mr. Perfect.' Yeah.
Sure. Right." — and then a long roll of Fiona's tired eyes,
and something muttered about "that two-faced schizoid shitdick."
That's the personal level. Culturally, it's A.D. 1400, and a cleric
scrubs his hands in rose-scent holy water, praises Our Lord,
then orders the thumbs of an errant ostler's assistant
severed "compleat at the joint." *The layers of sensibility
were in conflict,* as one textbook more tacitly puts it.
On a visible level it means a noblewoman could donate
jewels and time to an orphanage, yet that night could adorn
her hair with those pitiful thumbs as a joke. On the level of physics,
here's a photograph of Fiona and Deke in which they look
enamored. It was a trick of the light that was particle.
It was a trick of the light that was wave.

———————

The pack is hunting. Wait — make that "The worshipers
of Dionysus" are hunting in the woods; are bringing down
their human prey; and tearing off its limbs and singing and slobbering
over those raw nubs. The textbook caption: *Example
of ecstasy.* / Centuries, many centuries, later
a girl is brought to the village priest. Wait — make that
a "girl." She *looks like* a girl, though only walks
(adroitly) on all fours, she must be six and yet her only speech
is yelping. She was found in a cave, in her own shit
and the fresh shit of a wolf, and now this gentle man
must take her to his home and gently make her only one
of her two selves. "My child," he says — as if she were his daughter.
If a priest could have a daughter, if his daughter
had a mouth that howled unstoppably at the full of the moon.

———————

And then on page 800 she isn't a cheap bar floozie
anymore (albeit one with demonstrated dignity): a birthmark
is uncovered under circumstances strikingly described, and she
spends two last chapters living as a duchess. Which is
also the saga of Al, the class schlemiel, who we soon learn
knows the oath that turns him into Captain Universe,
which is also the saga of—look in the mirror,
you'll see. Look out the window. The story of *anybody*
includes one great connective ligament of true Chang-Engian mystery.
We can see an incipient glimmer of it everywhere.
According to the *Saudi Gazette*, the eyes of Sharia,
a seven-year-old, "change color according to which dress she puts on,
blue, yellow, red, etc." As if her other, secret, interior shes
peek out of the public one.

It's twilight in the village—it's a viscous mix of equal
day and night. The priest looks in at his difficult charge,
his squirming wolf/girl as she sleeps her inscrutable sleep
in the bed below a carven figure of the thorned and nailed
man/god on the wall. And though he looks long, and he isn't
short on pensive contemplation of these two
antipodean beings for whom he feels such affection,
neither the tragedy nor the glory of them—or of any of us—
gets clarified under his gentle, uncensorious stare.
Fiona, for example. After legal fees to Pluto and back,
last-minute they *aren't* getting divorced. Deke, she says,
is difficult—but necessary. Go figure. *I* can't.
"And so I suppose you saw him last night?" And then,
with the eye-roll: "Yeah. Both of him."

What he was, he was a 'wanderer' [shaman initiate],
he walked alone in the forest, he spoke to invisible ones,
he fell to the ground and beat at his head, his eyes,
until he saw the far places. Many times, he did this.
And because of this he welcomed the gods. They accepted him,
they made him into a wolf, he fought like a wolf,
his food, his love, he took the way a wolf does.
When they were done and he was a person again, the gods
set his head on a flat rock, so he watched them
eat the flesh from his bones, he watched from outside of his body
as they cleaned his bones, and then they restored the flesh
and then the head. Because of this, what he is, among us
he is a healer. His soul can fly to the gods and bring back
'sickness rainbow' [healing powers], *and so we praise him.*

Sometimes you drive at night, the houses left and right
no more than blurs upon the night, the stars a speeding surface
streaked unreadably—as if you're traveling up a vein
in an alien body. This is when you understand you're capable
of anything, the *you* of you could fill whatever shape
the night provided. . . . / "Varro (116–27 B.C.) believed,
like most of his contemporaries, that bees could be
descended from bees *or* from rotting carcasses of oxen."
Maybe this is the poem that asks to be a rationale
for things I've done—for blots upon the rest
of what I am—that make me shameful. I did
those things; and I didn't. A part of me did them,
a bee of me, that unlike the others was born of a rotting ox,
and flew directly away from the promise of light and honey.

Her Literal One

As for the light—it was a city light
as I was a city ten-year-old, a flower that was actually
half weed, a scraggly Jewbloom on the north side of Chicago,
call it Scaredy-blossom, Bookhead, Clinging Wondereyes;
whatever, the light and I sufficed, although the dingy bloat
they call a sky there wasn't anybody's standard idea
of island-paradise blue, and I was nobody's notion
of first-prize hothouse exotica. The seasons turned,
a wheel at a carnival booth: some sucker-you win
and a lot more sucker-you lose. In a family
photograph album: nodding, waxily pallid heads
of Indian Pipe, like lackeys in obsequious salaams;
but also the Buddha-ly bulbous bodies
of Skunk Cabbage, confident, radiating a *thereness*.
This was Chicago, remember; tailpipes in winter
offered great gray blossoms showier than anything
in a horticultural text. I like particularly the ones
with double lives, so that March Marigold
is also Cowslip; Bouncing Bet is Soapwort;
Spotted Joe-Pye Weed is Gravelroot; Fire Pink
is Catchfly. As for sex—the nectary woo
of the *Habenaria* Orchid is engineered
so that the pixilated bee, on exiting
that clever sanctum, manages to pull the entire pollen sac
along with it, so fertilizes the next free Orchid it enters.
The fur of an animal is sex for them, a cotton sock,
the wind. Sex is an engine that powers us even
in repression: think of the passion elevated
out of a nun, think of the one emphatic annual flower
worn like a boutonniere by the Desert Cactus.
I grew, I was dew and sap. The seasons turned,
a tire on a drum to check for a puncture: what
was this one, maybe my mother's grave, my father's,
my divorce. And as for love—I wouldn't say "evergreen"

was the word, although love reappeared on a semiregular basis
in a sticky burst of the pistil and the stamen that we
long ago incorporated inside ourselves the way we did
the sea. In a family photograph album: the one in a snood;
the one elucidating a point; the lank vamp
and her sumo beau; the famished epicurean . . .
they're all here, in their hoed rows
or their potting soil—sometimes you can see a mass of leaves
snap up at the sun like a school
of piranha crazy on blood. So many—Thoreau says
the Virginia Meadow Beauty looks like
"a little cream pitcher." I've always thought that
Yellow Lady's Slipper looked less like footwear
and more like a saddle canteen that might be sized
to one of the plastic horses from my Fort Apache set
when I was six. The yellow stamens
of the Fragrant Water Lily look like blasts from the hell
of the fundamentalists, shot through vents in the planet's surface.
The quiet white star that we've named Wood Anemone
reminds me of the fading of a bass chord,
given a visible body. Arrowhead is also
Duck Potato. Touch-Me-Not is also Jewelweed,
and its bilateral petals droop like golden testicles.
Forget-Me-Not is Mouse-Ear. But we *do* forget:
the seasons turn, unchanged; but, for their passengers,
the stars bear down like an emery wheel,
grinding away. And as for death—if even
Shakespeare and Dante acquiesced, who are *we* to say no?
As for death—traditionally, Jews visiting graves
set stones there as memoria, instead of flowers;
after all, why pretend? A gravel quarry
at the edge of a Jewish cemetery serves us for a florist,
and I like the hard idea of a dozen little stones
for a bouquet. I hope I haven't overlooked the pink idea
of the vulvas that a man knows in his lifetime
as a privilege, as a kind of lush botanical display.
As for the spirit—I hope I haven't neglected the gospel
lifting invisibly from the Calla Lily's throat. Yes,
as for the spirit—I remember an afternoon
when sun had touched, had brought alive, a church's

stained-glass Eden scene, and fifty members of the choir,
with their white robes stained deep green by this, all
turned to face that shining as if they
were phototropic. I *swear* a petal of Canadian Dwarf Cinquefoil
is, assuming my astronomy book is accurate, the visual twin
of the radiation emitted by a white dwarf star
four thousand light-years from Earth. As for remarriage,
Skyler is kneeling outside right now in her floppy
shade hat, with her hand rake and her spade.
As for my students—this is metaphor at work,
applied with a bricklayer's trowel, and then happily
pile-drivered into place. Do you see
how mimetic it is, of the frail *us* that wakes with us,
inside us, every day to meet whatever random
nurturing or savaging the light is going to do?
As for my wife—this is my garden, this is the best
I can tend, while she's all sweat and song and bent
to the difficult needs of her literal one.

January 31, 1998

The week I turn fifty, the President's busy
earnestly deflecting the taint of another sex encounter
in an alcove off the Oval Office: *"earnestly,"* we'd write it
if we didn't believe him; if we do, we'd carat-in
alleged in front of *sex.* / It's 1500
in the book of Chinese watercolors: scholar-artist T'ang Yin
is asleep inside his mountain cottage, dreaming that a self of him,
that looks like him, is floating in the air above
the highest peaks, that looks like air we'd have
if lakes of milk gave off a vapor. / And in world news:
all of the usual saucers swoop their usual aerial maneuvers
overhead, as if the world could press the sky
the way we do our eyes, until it calls forth patterns;
over Buenos Aires; Suffolk; Wayne, New Jersey. /
My aunt is doing better: she calls from San Diego, and kibbitzes
weather and health: she's eighty-six, however,
dwindling kidneys, silt-filled heart: this, sadly, earns
a qualifying touch (*My aunt is doing "better"*). /
At Alex's MFA cello recital, there was a moment
he rested his head upon that great round wooden shoulder
. . . he shut his eyes, he was so *small* against the music,
and so trusting of it . . . he looked like an infant
sweetly being patted free of spit-up. / And in local news:
the never-ending battle over hog-farm zoning.
(This being Kansas, one day it replaces
the illegal stockpiling of nerve gas by Iraq
as front-page headline.) / The week I turn fifty,
Judith gifts me with a book called *Offbeat Museums:*
The Hamburger Hall of Fame, The Museum of Bathroom Tissue.
Most are devoted, it seems, to preserving something just about
to slip off the edge of existence: the tools of the country physician
(leech jars, bleeding bowls, a "Vapo-cresoline Inhaler"),
or the fluffy scanties of old-time burlesque. Is this a hint
from Judith? Am I starting on the downslope

into relichood? / My one lame contribution
to the wealth of talk-show quasi-witticisms: "Oh yeah,
the President—I *told* him that this would catch up with him,
sooner or fellater." And, more seriously,
the relentless public discussion of: what *should* properly
be the domain of "public discussion"?—as if a problem, in being
self-consciously a problem, might lead to solution. /
Half-a-century. I say it. I say it again.
It's on my tongue all week,
like a sliver of blowfish: eventually
it will be fatal, but first . . . a tingly and addictive pleasure
overcomes the gourmet. / If I remember my tabloid facts correctly,
Arnold Schwarzenegger, Goldie Hawn, and Farah Fawcett
are also fifty, or may have slipped off the edge of fifty,
into fifty-one. (For fans of mine in the late-late twenty-first century
who don't recognize those names: they were "stars"
in what we once called "movies." Like the "real" stars,
they used themselves up in shining.) / "Albert"
means *all bright*: my angels (the "Angels of Light")
are Isaac, Gabriel, Mithra, Shamshiel. One weird day
in this week of bitter winter sky the color of rotten catfish,
glorious suds of a golden afternoon sun upbubble
from that grim gray slop, and light falls for an hour,
new light trembling into old light. There should be a museum
of dead light on display. (Well, that's
what photographs are.) / "As a young man,
he was given to drinking, and led an unconventional life"
—T'ang Yin. He's walking over the delicate catsback-arches
of the bridges in the Ming dynasty, and through its knobby hills,
he's thinking, rendering a poem of his from less
to even better less: a kind of freighted brevity
that I admire since, needless to say (but you see?
I'm saying it *anyway*), it's not *my* métier.
By the time he gets home, it's reduced to two lines: "Rooster":
All of its life, it only makes a few utterances;
But when it does, ten thousand doors bang open. /
[I'm looking now at my scribbled notes. It might not
have been "brevity," but "beauty." Of course, in T'ang Yin
they're one.] / Fifty; and my aunt is eighty-six:
another distance she connects when San Diego rings

this telephone in Wichita, Kansas. Fannie,
Lou, and Irv are living presences again, and float
the wired air between us . . . and we're all
one undifferentiatable flesh. The law of thermodynamics
doesn't care whether I'm in a booth at Tabby's Topless Lounge,
or in the family ground at Waldheim Cemetery in west Chicago.
"How are *you* feeling, kiddo?" asks my aunt.   /   The friend report
for the week of my birthday: Kim's lump
is benign. Flinn *isn't* going to take the job in Cairo.
Lisa and Terry—the 24-hour flu. Dawn stayed the night
with Kev, but Saralee showed up while they were, you know,
indisposed. Regina received bouquets from *three* admirers.
No one walks unshaken from the bad breath of a sudden conversation
with Mortality: for two days, Kim is a weeping mess
with her good news clutched to her breast.   /   *A circling plane,*
like the control bar
for our marionettish prancing here on the earth.
That, from my notebook. On the same afternoon:
A flock of birds in flight, that turn
like louvers and redden with sunset.   /
One more drone-a-thon committee meeting
here at Central Mediocre U. A hundred ways to reinterpret
"and" or "but." A hundred civilized procedures
for the filthying of decency. Barbituate haze
claims most of us. There are others, a few, who thrive in this
thick matrix. (Then again, there are seeds
evolved especially to germinate in certain types of dung.)   /
Iraq continues being a petulant threat. The thought
of fatal, unstoppable chemical clouds let loose
can douse a good mood in an eyeblink. I remember
during an earlier "international crisis" arguing
in our friendly way: David and Barbara Clewell,
Don Finkel, Connie Urdang: Connie saying
her generation lived through World War II and its atomic implications,
so she no longer believed the entire planet was ever doomed,
no matter how grave an individual circumstance. And five years later
David and Barbara are long divorced, and Connie
dead of cancer. "The entire planet" (for now) survives.   /
"Cancer"—we're afraid to even say it or write it;
"tumor"; "cyst." Afraid the gods would overhear

and meddle, in their dark way. Best to let the gods
remain on their mountain.   /   Speaking of which,
the *London Sunday Times* reports the Hong Kong paper *Ta Kung Pao*
reports that "people in China are eating the dried flesh
of celestial beings, convinced that this prevents cancer." Now
that would make a bodacious export! (Also a great
stock market tip.)   /   Not everybody is yielding
to entropy: in world news, Constance Driscoll, eighty-four,
eloped with Charles Barnes, her "ninety-two-year-old lothario."
"I just wanted to be with the woman I love."   /
The Kam Wah Chung & Co. Museum preserves
(more accurately, *is*) that eastern Oregon, turn-of-the-century
pharmacy/sundries store-religious center-opium den
where Chinese immigrant laborers congregated in the Gold Rush years.
Slipping off the edge of recognition. . . . We can see
(for now) the pillow on which Ing Hay would take
a patient's pulse, and the tins of his herbal-cure ingredients:
bear paws, rattlesnake, chicken gizzards, tiger's bone,
dried lizards, and a variety of animal gall bladders.
Mousetraps. Mining equipment. Peanut butter. Incense.
And the papered walls of the four-bunk room in back
look so *immediately* black, for a second
you think you're in the living lung
of one of the doped-up dreamers of 1898.   /   In world news:
snipers; hunger; racketeering; and a waterstain
in the shape of the Blessed Virgin Mary
that's already healed (*allegedly* healed) two
ovarian maladies, a gunshot wound, "the rectal itch."   /
January. Fifty.
Winter cold and dark, cold and dark,
and my own small rolled-up hedgehog ball of warmth.   /
The friend report: C. K. is going to have a surgical tube
inserted up his penis. Flinn *might* go to Cairo after all,
in any case he's letting them fly him out to San Francisco
for the interview: farewell, adieu. Mark Cox
unboxes a set of physician's saddlebags,
tattered and redolent, from the midrange 1800s,
looking just like the ones on page 56 in *Oddball Museums*:
two brown mounds, and in their leathery air
are the fussily twine-tied paper packets

and wax-sealed vials of an earlier pharmacopoeia than ours.
(My wife reminds me that the book in which they're pictured is,
as object—"book"—about as outmoded now
as the tiny marble mortar and pestle a doctor once carried.) Also
Judith Taylor calls to say the L.A. hills are turning ever
dangerous in this year's rains; she's had her house protected
by construction of a temporary berm. That's lovely language
and I'd like to write a book about our sad, sweet lives
called *Temporary Berm.* / From my notebook:
Kids fall onto the lawn, and meet their own shadows
like scissors closing. Later: *Newton's laws*
spruced up for a decadent era: matter and energy
french kiss. And later: *My aunt is going,*
slowly, steadily. Where does she go?
As if it's an answer, a few pages further:
New snow, into old snow. / The cold dry climate,
the stone exterior—these assured that decades after,
when Kam Wah Chung & Co. was unboarded in 1969, its tins
of algae and turtle shell, its ornate Chinese chest, were held
as ready as any other powerful memory
to be brought into the present. . . . I think of the way
that yellow barrier-tape police use at a crime scene
keeps its objects from the flow of time, inviolate, yet
waiting for renewed attention. Cribbage boards.
Hotel spittoons. Mercury bullets for syphilis.
"Lumbago remedy" syrups. The office mimeograph.
(Some memories, of course, are more emphatically guarded over
than that: across the taste of the tissues
of our mothers' wombs, the birthed mind sets an X
of flaming swords in the hands of wingéd sphinxes. Hollywood
films make use of a "continuity person"—someone
overseeing the look of a rouged cheek or a makeupped bruise
from scene to scene—but there's no psychic
"continuity hormone" that can thread me backward
fifty years and nine months, through the fur-me,
and the bird-me, to the first meiotic moment. By the way,
does anybody at the end of the twenty-first century remember
Steve McQueen?—a rough-and-tumble, hunky, blondly handsome,
charismatic he-man movie star who died
at fifty.) / Local news: a body's found

in Afton Lake. Alms
in a beggar's bowl, circling, crying
more, more, more.   /   In local news, in national news . . .
by week's end it's too difficult to separate the punchy stink
of hog farms from the odor that attends each further breakthrough
on the presidential sexcapades. The two get too
confused. *Too much!* my hissily steaming
muchómeter says as the week creeps into its danger zone.
A Bigfoot sighting . . . *stop!* A dram of sickly green plutonium
the authorities confiscated . . . *stop!* I really mean
that Bigfoot was *allegedly* sighted . . . *stop* BUZZ *stop.*   /
The friend report: Kim gives me *The National Catholic
Farm Life Conference Guide,* which includes the Church's
"Blessing of a Dynamo" and the "Blessing of Lard and Bacon."
What a world!   /   The friend report: Stephen says
in dust-bowl days, the sand was driven with force enough
to saw through fence posts. Nathan says
his father, when he was an infant, was set in a shoe box,
then the shoe box in an oven, to protect him
from the dust storms of the 1930s.   /   The friend report:
Jo is pregnant again, a happy thing. (The first time, the fetus
strangled in its umbilical cord. I've heard a dozen people say
"born dead"—*can* those two words be paired?)   /   The friend report:
Lisa gives me homemade cookies. Rita, a great blue
M&Ms dispenser [editor: footnote,
for the sake of the farther edge of the twenty-first century].
Kathleen D., a painting she's done, of a fuchsia raygun. Nobody
brings me any tacky stupid funereal
"Over the Hill" gag gifts: I have good taste in friends.   /
The friend report: *stop, take that phone off the hook!*
(Those disconnected halves will only fuse together again,
like an earthworm.)   /   Local news: I'm suing
my employer, Central Mediocre U., for violating, repeatedly,
my due-process rights [which technically we still had
in the twentieth century: maybe you of the future
display them, mounted like dinos or dodos, in your museums].   /
Local news: a clutch of medical syringes
washes up on the shore of Afton Lake, a small but sharp discordance
in the night, like static gargled in a radio's throat.   /
Some *very* local news: a grackle circles overhead,

and keeps a supervisory eye on the block.   /   Some very, *very*
local news: that pinprick patch of tingle
just above my knee won't go away . . . I'm fifty.   /
When I step outside, I see my breath
rise up to burning patterns in the sky, still rolling
—dice shook fifty years ago.   /   *Enough.*   /   In 1948
A Streetcar Named Desire received the Pulitzer Prize,
and Auden did, and Michener, and the yield of white potatoes
in the United States by bushel was 446 million, and *cybernetics*
entered popular usage, and *shmoo,*
and, and . . . *Stop. Too much.* Too cargo'd a century.
The brain's evolved to lottery-pick
one winning fact from out of the revolving drum of chaos.
Let the rest of it slip off the edge of the world.   /
The friend report: "You're writing an eight-page poem
about your *birthday*? I've got *one* word for you:
e-g-o." (I can trust my friends to be honest. How nice.)
But—arbitrary constructs though they all are,
still it *isn't* the same to turn, say,
thirty, forty, forty-seven. . . . Someone else
somewhere is juicing out a robust harmonica blues about this.
Someone else is creating a figure called 50
from painted popsicle sticks and thread spools.
Everybody is sure his/her own one indispensable life is
"kam wah chung"—"desert flower"; or also
"golden flower of prosperity." I look up from my writing
at 7:44 A.M. on January 31st: a single string
inside me twangs a single note. And with that *plink,*
I sail across the International Me Line.   /
There's a photograph of my aunt
and my father; she must be nine or ten, that makes
the photograph's technology superceded
by three-quarters of a century. Their blackly sepia outfits
blend, as if they might be attached at the hip
by a living ligament. All of his life, they were truly
that close; and in his death
she feels close to him—she speaks of him,
and *to* him; and in *her* death, too,
whenever it comes, they'll both be disappearing
in the ground of Waldheim Cemetery, stage by stage,

until—like children again, in a race—she
catches up to his head start. I brought the picture with me
when I visited her last month. "Do you remember
Cousin Ruthie?" she asks. The presidents she's lived through
over eighty-six years are as nothing to her, are background hum,
but Cousin Ruthie gave her the bow in that photograph,
so lays claim to a presence that lingers
like lawn mist which will stay here as long
as my aunt does. "I love you" she tells me between
one IV tube and the next. This run-down century
has just two years remaining, but
the doctor says my aunt has less; I'll have to love her
into the next millennium without her.
When I leave she asks me to make a row of that photograph
and a handful of others, over the wall
that runs along her bedside
—temporary berm.   /   The week I turn fifty,
none of this is new. In 1500, these intrigues and griefs,
follies and devotions, insurrections and alliances, continue
undiminished from their first pre–*Homo sapiens* appearances,
and show no signs of waning. From the Everfloating Void
above our world, a human image slowly drifts back down
and joins its earthly body once again, reenters
days and nights of wine shop, scandal, lawyers
—for such (in part) is the life of T'ang Yin.
He's been dreaming. And now he's going to set it down
on a wafer of unrolled rice paper. Writing:
Rain on the river. That's all. That's his poem.
He's writing:

Rain on the river.